Perfectionism

Michael Brustein, PsyD, is a clinical psychologist currently in private practice in New York City and in New Jersey. He has previously been a supervising psychologist at the James J. Peters VA Medical Center in the Bronx, NY, mentoring psychology interns and medical residents. He has held an assistant professor position at Albert Einstein Medical School and been an attending psychologist at Montefiore Medical Center. He regularly consults with media and production companies assisting with plot and character development relating to mental health issues. Dr. Brustein has taught courses on abnormal psychology, theories of personality, psychotherapy techniques, group therapy, self-psychology, psychodynamics of substance abuse, and bereavement at William Paterson University, The College of New Rochelle, and Brooklyn College. Dr. Brustein is currently working on a series of self-help books.

Perfectionism:

A Guide for Mental Health Professionals

Michael Brustein, PsyD

SPRINGER PUBLISHING COMPANY
NEW YORK

Copyright © 2014 Springer Publishing Company, LLC

All rights reserved.

No part of this publication may be reproduced, stored in a retrieval system, or transmitted in any form or by any means, electronic, mechanical, photocopying, recording, or otherwise, without the prior permission of Springer Publishing Company, LLC, or authorization through payment of the appropriate fees to the Copyright Clearance Center, Inc., 222 Rosewood Drive, Danvers, MA 01923, 978-750-8400, fax 978-646-8600, info@copyright.com or on the Web at www.copyright.com.

Springer Publishing Company, LLC
11 West 42nd Street
New York, NY 10036
www.springerpub.com

Acquisitions Editor: Nancy Hale
Composition: Diacritech

ISBN: 978-0-8261-0610-0
e-book ISBN: 9780826106117

13 14 15 16 / 5 4 3 2 1

The author and the publisher of this Work have made every effort to use sources believed to be reliable to provide information that is accurate and compatible with the standards generally accepted at the time of publication. The author and publisher shall not be liable for any special, consequential, or exemplary damages resulting, in whole or in part, from the readers' use of, or reliance on, the information contained in this book. The publisher has no responsibility for the persistence or accuracy of URLs for external or third-party Internet websites referred to in this publication and does not guarantee that any content on such websites is, or will remain, accurate or appropriate.

Library of Congress Cataloging-in-Publication Data

Brustein, Michael (Michael A.), author.
  Perfectionism : a guide for mental health professionals / Michael Brustein.
      p. ; cm.
  Includes bibliographical references and index.
  ISBN 978-0-8261-0610-0 — ISBN 978-0-8261-0611-7 (e-book)
  I. Title.
  [DNLM: 1. Obsessive-Compulsive Disorder—psychology. 2. Achievement. 3. Cognitive Therapy—methods. 4. Obsessive-Compulsive Disorder—therapy. 5. Self Psychology. WM 176]
  RC533
  616.85'22706—dc23
                                    2013028153

Special discounts on bulk quantities of our books are available to corporations, professional associations, pharmaceutical companies, health care organizations, and other qualifying groups. If you are interested in a custom book, including chapters from more than one of our titles, we can provide that service as well.

For details, please contact:
Special Sales Department, Springer Publishing Company, LLC
11 West 42nd Street, 15th Floor, New York, NY 10036-8002
Phone: 877-687-7476 or 212-431-4370; Fax: 212-941-7842
E-mail: sales@springerpub.com

Printed in the United States of America by Gasch Printing.

Contents

Preface   *vii*

Acknowledgments   *ix*

1. Defining Perfectionism and Examining the Consequences   1
2. Therapeutic Alliance and Therapy Ruptures   17
3. Interpersonal Approach and Perfectionists   35
4. Self-Psychology and Perfectionism: Consolidation of One's Sense of Self   57
5. Klein, Perfectionism, and Internal Battles   77
6. Mindfulness and Buddhist-Influenced Techniques   93
7. Cognitive Therapy and Perfectionism   107
8. Conclusion: Major Themes in Treating Perfectionist Clients   117

References   *125*

Index   *131*

Preface

The idea to do a book on perfectionism originated in 2008, 2 years after I started my private practice in New York City. Reflecting on the type of patients I was seeing, I noticed an interesting commonality. A relatively substantial portion of my patients presented with extremely high standards for themselves or others. These patients were also prone to self-reproach or anger if they or others failed to meet their standards. In clinical terms they were perfectionists and undergoing significant distress. Additionally, they were extremely complicated to treat and engage.

Although numerous studies existed regarding perfectionism, few books or studies addressed how to best provide psychotherapy to these patients. In reviewing research by Gordon Flett and Paul Hewitt (2002) I began to understand that the trait of perfectionism can be prevalent in clinical populations because it predisposes individuals to numerous psychopathologies ranging from anxiety, depression, and personality disorders. In addition, I learned that my struggle with forming an alliance with perfectionists was not uncommon. Research (Zuroff et al., 2000) indicates that perfectionists are more difficult to form an alliance with than nonperfectionist patients.

Unfortunately, the few books and journal articles devoted to treating perfectionists were almost exclusively cognitive-behavioral in focus. Consequently, for my own edification and to fill in a void in psychological literature I decided to write this book. The book discusses the construct of perfectionism, the adaptive and maladaptive aspects of perfectionism and how it contributes to numerous psychological issues. The book primarily focuses on diverse relational approaches, such as self-psychological and interpersonal theories to understand, intervene, and work through the therapeutic ruptures clinicians may experience with perfectionists. Cognitive-behavioral approaches to use when working with perfectionist patients such as mindfulness are also discussed. Case studies are used extensively to illustrate how to apply these diverse frameworks to perfectionist patients. I have found having a flexible clinical perspective is highly important when working with perfectionists as they present with complex challenges and dynamics.

Michael Brustein, PsyD

Acknowledgments

My sincere thanks to Pam Amri and Philip Laughlin for their initial interest in working with me to develop this book. A special thank you to my editor, Nancy Hale, for her patience and encouragement throughout the process. I am grateful to my esteemed friends and colleagues who gave their time and insight into reviewing the text.

Thank you to my parents, Ellen and Larry Brustein, for your love and guidance. Most importantly, this book would not have been possible without the love and support of my wife, Jackie Lissy Brustein, and the light of our children, Jonah and Eve.

Perfectionism

ONE

Defining Perfectionism and Examining the Consequences

*Keep your eyes on the stars and your feet
on the ground.*

—Theodore Roosevelt

Over the past few decades, a great deal of research (Flett & Hewitt, 2002) has focused on studying the relationship between perfectionism and psychological adaption and disorders. The research demonstrates that perfectionism can be maladaptive and predispose individuals to depression, suicidality, anxiety, eating disorders, personality disorders, and numerous other psychiatric issues (Bastiani, Rao, Weltzin, & Kaye, 1995; Hewitt & Flett, 1993; Hewitt, Flett, & Turnbull, 1992; Hewitt, Flett, & Turnbull-Donovan, 1992; Juster et al., 1996).

Providing psychotherapy and treating individuals with perfectionist traits can be extremely difficult. This occurs for several reasons. For example, individuals with perfectionist traits can be hostile and critical when interacting with others; alternatively, they may be passive and withdrawn to avoid being seen negatively. The aggressive or avoidant state can make therapeutic engagement more difficult to establish.

Although a great number of studies have emerged examining the relationship between perfectionism and various disorders, few articles and books have focused on addressing how to best work therapeutically with perfectionist patients. This book covers several perspectives on treating perfectionist patients, ranging from psychodynamic to cognitive-behavioral approaches. This first chapter defines perfectionism and explores adaptive and maladaptive aspects of perfectionism. It takes a brief look at Steve Jobs and Bobby Knight, two highly successful leaders in their fields, and how perfectionism influenced their lives. The chapter illustrates how the trait of perfectionism can make someone vulnerable to several psychiatric disorders and can affect the treatment process and therapeutic alliance.

Chapter 2 discusses forming therapeutic alliances with perfectionist patients and provides different approaches to fostering the alliance and resolving therapeutic ruptures. Chapters 3 to 5 discuss working with the perfectionist from interpersonal, self-psychological, and Kleinian perspectives, respectively. Case examples on how to intervene and understand perfectionism from these perspectives are explored. Chapters 6 and 7 discuss working with patients from mindful and cognitive-behavioral approaches. Each approach adds a valuable lens and techniques facilitating how to effectively work with the challenging perfectionist patient.

DEFINING PERFECTIONISM

Perfectionism is now widely seen as a multidimensional construct. In this chapter, two multidimensional conceptualizations, by Hewitt and Flett (1991) and by Frost, Marten, Lahart, and Rosenblate (1990), are discussed.

Three-Component Conceptualization

One of the most popular and accepted conceptualizations of perfectionism was developed by Hewitt and Flett (1991) and Hewitt, Flett, Turnbull-Donovan, and Mikail (1991). In this conceptualization,

1. Defining Perfectionism and Examining the Consequences

perfectionism is broken down into three components: self-oriented perfectionism, socially oriented perfectionism, and other-oriented perfectionism. The different components of perfectionism have different psychological and social and behavioral consequences.

Self-oriented perfectionism consists of setting incredibly high personal standards. The standards set by perfectionists are often unrealistic. Their goals are not just to excel but to be perfect and to avoid failing at any cost. When they do not achieve their goals, self-oriented perfectionists can be highly self-critical, leading to distress. They often experience intense self-scrutiny about their performance across several domains.

When self-oriented perfectionists ostensibly achieve their goals, they may still experience disappointment. For example, athlete A, a self-oriented perfectionist who performed perfectly in a wrestling match, still feels dejected. The athlete, despite achieving his initial goal, may continue to be dissatisfied because he felt that he had to prepare more than appropriate or more than the ideal amount of time.

Socially oriented perfectionists have the exaggerated perception that everyone has excessively high standards for them. In reality, achieving these standards consistently may not be possible. If they do not meet these perceived high standards, socially oriented perfectionists believe they will not obtain approval, will endure rejection, or will lose acceptance. The excessively high standards that they experienced as being externally imposed can make them feel as though they are not in control but instead are helpless.

Other-oriented perfectionists have excessively high standards of other people. They can be highly critical of those who do not meet their demands or expectations. Other people are thus expected to be perfect. This pattern of behavior is essentially similar to self-oriented perfectionism but has been turned outward or externalized toward others. An example of this trait is seen in a person who yells excessively if someone else makes a mistake. A boss who punishes and shouts at employees for any shortcoming is another example of other-oriented perfectionism.

Six-Dimensional Conceptualization

In Frost et al.'s (1990) conceptualization of perfectionism, there are six dimensions:

1. Excessive concern over mistakes
2. Excessive high personal standards (e.g., must be the best)
3. High parental expectations (e.g., never feeling like parental standards are met)
4. Parental criticism (e.g., feelings pertaining to falling short of parental expectations)
5. Exaggerated emphasis on precision, order, and organization
6. Doubts about actions

The major dimensions of perfectionism associated with psychopathology are excessive concern over mistakes (Frost et al., 1990) and doubts about actions. There is an association between these two dimensions and social anxiety (Juster et al., 1996), depression (Enns, Cox, & Clara, 2005), and eating disorders (Bastiani et al., 1995). In addition, concern over mistakes and doubts about actions have a correlation with obsessive-compulsive issues (Rhéaume, Freeston, Dugas, Letarte, & Ladouceur, 1995).

Aspects of Frost's dimensions of perfection are associated with aspects of Flett and Hewitt's (2002) perfectionism construct. For instance, self-oriented perfectionism is most closely related to excessive high personal standards (Frost, Heimberg, Holt, Mattia, & Neubauer, 1993). Excessive concerns over mistakes, high parental expectations, and parental criticism are associated with socially oriented perfectionism (Frost et al., 1993).

PERFECTIONISM AND ADAPTION

An important question that arises is whether perfectionism is always maladaptive. Some researchers suggest components of perfectionism may be positive, such as high-striving or self-oriented perfectionism (Kilbert, Langhinrichsen-Rohling, & Saito, 2005). It appears logical that a person with high standards or goals would be motivated to achieve. Some research has shown that perfectionism has been associated with conscientiousness, self-efficacy, and satisfaction. (Nakano, 2009; Ulu & Teezer, 2010; Wang, Yeun, & Slaney, 2009). In addition, throughout history, many perfectionist individuals appear to have greatly and positively influenced our society.

Steve Jobs: Defining Success

Steve Jobs, who shaped the way we consume entertainment, communicate with one another, read, and organize our schedules, could be considered a perfectionist. His biographer, Walter Isaacson, states that his "passion for perfection and ferocious drive revolutionized six industries: personal computers, animated movies, music, phones, tablet computing, and digital publishing" (Isaacson, 2011, p. xx–xxi). Without Job's perfectionist traits, would he have accomplished as much as he did and have been as successful?

Jobs had intense strivings and did not settle for anything less than the ideals he had envisioned. For instance, Jobs forced the designers of the Mac operating system to redo the title bars at the top of the windows approximately 20 times until he was satisfied (Isaacson, 2011). His high ideals likely led to the sleek products to which our society has become extremely attached and covetous. Research indicates that there may be certain components of perfectionism that are adaptive (Stoeber & Otto, 2006). Perfectionist strivings are related to higher levels of conscientiousness, endurance, and active coping, which appear to be qualities Jobs possessed. With all of the positive achievements Jobs made ostensibly related to his perfectionism, were there negative ramifications?

Isaacson's biography suggests that Jobs spent time attempting to search for inner peace. Daniel Kottke, an early Apple employee and Jobs's friend, reported that Jobs "could not achieve inner calm" (Isaacson, 2011, p. 47). Perhaps Jobs experienced a lack of inner peace as a result of his perfectionist strivings. How did he respond when not meeting his goals? Did he feel distressed and unhappy? Jobs rarely discussed such personal responses, so we may never know the answers to these questions.

Although speculative, perfectionism may have led Jobs to make decisions that shortened his life. When diagnosed with pancreatic cancer, he initially denied the recommended treatment and opted to postpone surgery, veering toward more holistic remedies (Isaacson, 2011). Nine months later he did decide to undergo surgery; however, by that time, his cancer had spread. He later regretted not obtaining the surgery. Did issues with control and overinvestment in his rigid ideals about what he could achieve on his own hamper his capacity to follow medical recommendations? Did an active coping style associated with positive strivings affect his capacity to take a more passive role letting medical doctors steer his treatment? The answers remain unclear.

Other negative ramifications from Jobs's perfectionism appear to be in social realms. In addition to having extremely high ideals for himself and what he produced, he held others to exceptionally harsh standards as well. His eulogy given by his sister notes that he went through 67 nurses before he found 3 whom he liked (*New York Times*, 10/30/2011). He was extremely difficult to work with and devaluing toward others, referring to his former fellow employees at Atari as "dumb shits" (Isaacson, 2011, p. 42). Andy Hertzfield, a member of the team that developed the first Apple Macintosh computer, stated "the one question I'd truly love Steve to answer is, 'Why are you sometimes so mean?'" (Isaacson, 2011, p. 564). At the same time, Jobs was respected, and many people were quite fond of him.

Overall, Jobs appeared to have elements of self- and other-oriented perfectionism. In some ways his perfectionism likely led to great innovations. His high perfectionist strivings and goals led him to refine his work until he achieved elegant products. However, his need for control and his active coping style in situations he couldn't control, such as his medical issues, may have not been adaptive. In addition, his hostility associated with other-oriented perfectionism may have led to strained relationships. His lack of inner peace may have been associated with concerns over mistakes, which research illustrates is associated with negative aspects of perfectionism.

Bobby Knight: Rejecting Failure

Like Jobs, Bobby Knight, the famous former coach of the Indiana Hoosiers men's college basketball team, is a renowned individual whose behavior is consistent with perfectionism, particularly self- and other-oriented perfectionism. Failure to Knight was intolerable, and losing destroyed his identity. Steve Alford, a former Indiana player, referred to Knight's holy grail as the game in which mistakes did not occur. If the team lost a game, players who Knight felt were responsible were excluded from riding back home with the rest of the team (Dweck, 2012). Knight believed they did not deserve respect. He would call players "pussies" and once put a tampon in a player's locker to illustrate this point (Dweck, 2012). He was feared by players who did not want to experience his harsh judgment and rage.

Knight had impressive success as a coach, winning three National Collegiate Athletic Association (NCAA) championships. Were his tactics, high expectations of winning, and high standards for others on his team adaptive? Although he had success, many players struggled under his system and described the atmosphere as poisonous (Dweck, 2012). Alford said he lost zest for the sport at times. Isiah "Zeke" Thomas, a former Indiana University player who went on to have an impressive National Basketball Association (NBA) career before he retired, expressed that at times he would have shot Knight if he had had a gun and other times he would have hugged him (Dweck, 2012). What would have happened if Knight had held on to his high expectations but decreased his punitive stance toward what he saw as failures by others and by himself? Would he have gotten even more out of players by helping them grow? Could he have been another John Wooden, the former record-setting head coach at University of California at Los Angeles, and won 10 championships?

As mentioned, researchers suggest that maladaptive perfectionism occurs when someone becomes highly critical when goals are not achieved (Melrose, 2011). The next section discusses in more detail perfectionism and maladaptation consequences to which the trait can lead.

PERFECTIONISM AND MALADAPTATION

Studies indicate that perfectionism is a trait that can predispose people to depression and anxiety due to how perfectionists perceive and cope with events and their social environment (Dunkley, Blankstein, Halsall, Williams, & Winkworth, 2000; Hewitt & Flett, 1993; Juster et al., 1996). In addition, perfectionists' self-concept and cognitive style (e.g., ruminative tendencies) are associated with depression (O'Connor, O'Connor, & Marshall, 2007). Depression is classified as an Axis I disorder in the American Psychiatric Association's *Diagnostic and Statistical Manual of Mental Disorders* (1994). It is also is associated with Axis II personality disorders and a self-presentation style that can be problematic in forming therapeutic alliances.

Research conducted by Hewitt and Flett (1993) suggests that self-oriented perfectionists are prone to perceiving events that get in the way of their achievement goals as hassles. Research by Dunkley et al. (2000) contends that perfectionists with concerns over mistakes (a dimension associated with socially oriented perfectionism) are prone to experiencing more daily hassles and consequently depression and anxiety. It can be conjectured that this occurs because of the perfectionist's rigid belief or perception that nothing can or should go wrong. An obligation or delay (e.g., social or work related) may be interpreted catastrophically by a perfectionist and seen as more intrusive or deleterious to goals than it actually is. Minor setbacks may be perceived as major failures, leading to depression and feelings of incompetence.

In addition, studies indicate that perfectionists, particularly socially oriented perfectionists (e.g., with concerns over mistakes), engage in maladaptive strategies when coping with stressors or hassles, which contributes to depression. (Dunkley et al., 2000; Harding, Hewitt, & Flett, 2003). For example, perfectionists with concerns over mistakes may engage in avoidant strategies, feeling hopeless about their efficacy and capacity to solve problems. As a result, problems remain unresolved, exacerbating their negative mood state.

Research by Sherry, Law, Hewitt, Flett, and Besser (2008) illustrates that socially oriented perfectionists also perceive a lack of social support (e.g., feelings of close attachment), which makes them prone to feeling socially disconnected and depressed. This perception regarding social support may stem from beliefs that they are unable to live up to others' extreme expectations. Feeling disconnected and unaccepted by others may cause socially oriented perfectionists to act in adverse ways, such as withdrawing or engaging in a hostile behavior. Theoretically, this behavior can then induce others to withdraw support. The Sherry et al. (2008) study did not illustrate that socially oriented perfectionists actually received less social support. However, the study lacked a longitudinal design, and the social support perfectionists receive may degrade over time.

Socially oriented perfectionists' proneness to perceiving others as not accepting may stem from lack of self-acceptance. Research illustrates that self-, socially, and other-oriented perfectionists lack unconditional self-worth (Flett, Besser, Davis, & Hewitt, 2003). Unconditional self-worth is having positive self-regard regardless of social acceptance or personal achievements. A person with unconditional self-worth can fail at a task or endure social rejection and still remain positive about him- or herself. It can be postulated that when a person feels confident, he or she is less preoccupied, sensitive, or reliant on approval from others. Consequently, when not receiving positive feedback, the person would be less prone to negative mood states. Studies indicate that low unconditional self-worth is associated with perfectionism, as well as with depression (Flett et al., 2003).

Other factors related to perfectionism and depression are cognitive styles, specifically rumination. Rumination acts as a mediator with perfectionist individuals, leading to psychological difficulties such as depression and anxiety (O'Connor et al., 2007). Rumination and brooding consist of continuously thinking about negative experiences. Studies indicate that self- and socially oriented perfectionists are prone to this process and likely are replaying shortcomings or flaws regarding personal or social achievements (O'Conner et al., 2007). The rumination that leads to distress may also consist of cognitions that are not related to perfectionistic cognitions.

Perfectionists are prone to rumination to obtain a sense of control over failing to live up to expectations. The replaying of events may function as a way to master or undo negative events or trajectories. The perfectionist may replay thoughts and events in the hope a solution will emerge (O'Connor et al., 2007). This mechanism is often maladaptive, because the replaying of negative events amplifies negative affective states.

Although both socially and self-oriented perfectionism are related to rumination, there is a stronger connection between socially oriented perfectionism and rumination. This may be because meeting the expectations of others may be perceived as being less under the control of socially oriented perfectionists, who rely on the approval of others rather than personal accomplishments. The lack of perceived control thus leads to increased rumination and subsequent amplified distress, such as depression or anxiety.

PERFECTIONISTIC SELF-PRESENTATION AND PERSONALITY DISORDERS

A perfectionist's interpersonal or self-presentation style may also be a vulnerability factor that makes perfectionists prone to distress (Hewitt et al., 2003) and personality disorders. As mentioned, a perfectionist's underlying motive is to obtain perfection in either social or achievement realms. The self-presentation style is thus a separate but overlapping construct often superimposed on perfectionism. In essence, perfectionistic self-presentation is the communication of perfection to others influenced by one or more of the multidimensional motives of perfectionism. Perfectionistic self-presentation consists of three factors: self-promotion (proactively promoting a perfect image), nondisclosure of imperfection (e.g., concern over verbal disclosure of imperfection), and nondisplay of imperfection (concern about behavioral displays of imperfection; Hewitt et al., 2003).

Research illustrates that perfectionism in general is correlated with personality disorders (Sherry, Hewitt, Gordon, Lee-Baggley, & Hall, 2007). In particular, self-oriented perfectionism is associated with compulsivity, a trait consistent with obsessive-compulsive personality disorder. Other-oriented perfectionism is associated with externalizing personality pathology (cluster B), which consists of entitled, domineering, dramatic, and aggressive behavioral patterns (Sherry et al., 2007). These interpersonal behaviors are consistent with antisocial and narcissistic personality disorders. When needs or expectations are not met, other-oriented perfectionists react punitively.

Socially oriented perfectionism is associated with emotional dysregulation deficits, which coincide with borderline personality disorder (cluster B) (Sherry et al., 2007). Perfectionists have a schema that others expect perfection and are unfair and demanding. This schema can consequently contribute to resentment, angry outbursts, and hostility. Alternatively, socially oriented perfectionism is related to interpersonal anxiety and dependency (cluster C) consistent with avoidant and dependent personality pathology. Socially oriented perfectionists may gravitate toward dominant others and act submissive to those who have high expectations.

It can be conjectured that the self-presentation of perfectionists with personality pathology is to promote perfections and avoid disclosing imperfections, thus creating a false façade (Sherry et al., 2007). Individuals with narcissistic and borderline pathology (cluster B) have unstable identities. Through self-presentation behaviors, such as outwardly promoting a perfect image, they bolster inadequacies and attempt to elicit verification of perfection. In addition, nondisclosure protects perfectionists with avoidant or dependent (cluster C) personality pathology associated with socially oriented perfectionism from rejection. Ultimately, the self-presentation of perfectionists is an attempt to minimize distress in the long term, which may perpetuate interpersonal issues. Lack of direct communication or hiding needs can lead to lack of resolution in relationships.

INTIMATE AND THERAPY RELATIONSHIPS

Research indicates that, in general, perfectionism is associated with difficulties in interpersonal relationships, such as intimate and therapy relationships (Harding et al., 2003). Research conducted by Hewitt, Flett, and Mikail (1995) illustrates that patients under stress (chronic pain in the study) have lower levels of marital satisfaction if they have partners with elevated other-oriented perfectionism.

Other studies indicate that socially oriented perfectionism may also negatively affect marital relationships (Harding et al., 2003). Wives who displayed socially oriented perfectionism were found to inaccurately believe that their significant other requires perfection from them and to engage in a range of negative coping styles (e.g., avoidance, spending more time with friends, and conflict).

It can be speculated that women's use of negative coping strategies such as avoidance may be a way to protect against rejection, failure, or both. This strategy, however, leads to poorer marital functioning, most likely because ruptures are not repaired or addressed.

In addition, socially oriented husbands who believe that their wives require perfection from them tended to use mostly conflict strategies (e.g., sarcasm, nagging, and blaming) as a way of managing difficulties. The socially oriented husband, for example, may perceive the neutral request to clean the kitchen as a criticism indicating a failure. This could lead to the husband using aggressive sarcasm, feeling slighted, and believing that nothing he does will please his wife. This aggressive response likely causes a further rift in the marital dynamic (Harding et al., 2003).

In a therapy relationship, the role of perfectionism appears to negatively affect the therapeutic alliance and the outcome of the therapy relationship. For example, research by Hewitt, Habke, Lee-Baggley, Sherry, and Flett (2008) indicates that individuals with perfectionistic self-presentation display greater distress before a clinical interview, have higher negative expectations, and have more post interview dissatisfaction. Specifically, the need to avoid imperfections was associated with seeing the interviewer as threatening before and after the interview.

As another example, a study by Zuroff et al. (2000) illustrates that patients high in perfectionism did not increase their capacity to strengthen the therapeutic alliance as therapy progressed. Perfectionists also did not show significant clinical improvement. One explanation may be that a motivation to avoid imperfections may make perfectionists less likely to engage in an open and collaborative relationship as therapy progresses. Another explanation may be that as therapy progresses, perfectionists may respond to therapy ruptures poorly. This may be because they are employing maladaptive and avoidant strategies. Consequently, without resolving ruptures, the therapeutic alliance may not grow stronger.

Research stemming from the Treatment of Depression Collaborative Research Program (TDCRP) sponsored by the National Institute of Mental Health indicates that before treatment, perfectionists' relationship to negative outcomes is associated with their ability to establish quality social support systems (Shahar, Blatt, Zuroff, Krupnick, & Sotsky, 2004). Thus, the perfectionist patient's difficulties in the therapy relationship parallel and replicate problems the patient has in his or her social world. This offers some support for the concept of perfectionists experiencing negative transference toward the therapist.

Overall, the research from the TDCRP indicates that highly perfectionist patients do not benefit from brief interventions or medications in comparison to low- or middle-level perfectionist patients (Blatt, Zuroff, Quinlan, & Pilkonis, 1996). High-level perfectionists fail to benefit from brief interventions regardless of whether they have a positive perception of their therapist early on in the therapy relationship. This is because patients with high levels of perfectionism have intensely negative mental representations of themselves and others that take extensive time to work through. Research appears to indicate that longer-term therapy to alter the ingrained personality issue is most valuable.

Although studies conducted by Blatt and colleagues (e.g., Blatt et al., 1996; Shahar et al., 2004) and stemming from the TDCRP are helpful, perfectionism was measured in the program by the dysfunctional attitude scale, which provides a perfectionism or self-criticism factor but does not assess self-oriented, socially oriented, or other-oriented perfectionism. In the future, more precise research and outcome measures using Flett and Hewitt's (2002) construct of perfectionism would be beneficial. Nonetheless, the research provides some guidelines for how to proceed therapeutically.

Long-term therapy during which perfectionists can have the time and space to develop a therapeutic alliance may be most beneficial for perfectionist patients. Through the process of longer-term interpersonal, self-psychological, and psychodynamic therapies, perfectionists can develop less punitive mental representations. In addition, cognitive techniques and mindfulness can help reduce some problematic symptoms. For example, mindfulness and cognitive-behavioral therapy approaches (described in Chapters 6 and 7, respectively) can be extremely helpful for perfectionists in dealing with rumination and learning to accept limitations. Mindfulness can help perfectionists be less sensitive to emotional triggers when they feel they have fallen short. Cognitive restructuring can also help perfectionists manage unrealistic thoughts more successfully. The rest of this book gives a well-rounded approach to addressing a multifaceted problem.

TWO

Therapeutic Alliance and Therapy Ruptures

Out of perfection nothing can be made. Every process involves breaking something up.

—Joseph Campbell

The therapeutic alliance is one of the most important variables that predicts positive outcomes when working with psychotherapy patients. Establishing a positive therapeutic alliance can be particularly difficult with patients who struggle with perfectionism. This chapter defines the therapeutic alliance and explores particular challenges that perfectionist patients have when forming a positive alliance. Techniques are discussed on how to foster an alliance with perfectionist patients and manage therapy ruptures.

THERAPEUTIC ALLIANCE

Various definitions have been proffered for *therapeutic alliance*. This book uses Bordin's (1979) definition, which states that the three core interdependent elements of the therapeutic alliance are tasks, goals, and the therapeutic bond. Let's briefly consider each element in turn.

The tasks of a therapeutic alliance consist of specific activities that the patient must engage in to obtain benefits from the therapy. These tasks differ depending on the type of therapy delivered. For example, in cognitive-behavioral therapy, the tasks may include homework and cognitive restructuring. In psychodynamic therapy, the tasks may include free association or identifying relationship patterns. The goals of therapy constitute the general objective. In cognitive-behavioral therapy, the goal may be to develop more adaptive thoughts. Conversely, in psychodynamic therapy, the goal may be for the patient to have a more variegated interpersonal style. Last, the bond is the affective component of the relationship regarding whether the patient feels understood, respected, and valued. The bond affects the patient's capacity to negotiate tasks and goals.

As discussed in the previous chapter, research suggests perfectionist patients have more difficulty building collaborative therapy relationships compared with nonperfectionist patients, leading to poorer outcomes among the perfectionist patient population. In a study by Zuroff et al. (2000), subjects with perfectionistic tendencies did not differ from nonperfectionists in feeling valued and accepted by their therapists (perceived quality of the therapy relationship) in the course of short-term therapy. However, by the third session, perfectionists had failed to increase their contribution to the alliance and their engagement to their therapist. The researchers suggest that the lack of therapeutic engagement may result from potential limits in the capacity that perfectionists have to develop open and collaborative relationships.

Why do perfectionists have difficulty forming collaborative relationships? Shame and ambivalence about presenting vulnerabilities or concerns about control are two likely possibilities. To address these issues and foster a collaborative environment, there are several techniques and principles to consider. One important component to enhance the therapeutic alliance and reduce shame is psychoeducation or explaining the rationale behind the therapeutic approach. This is typically done in cognitive-behavioral therapy; it is also used in psychodynamic therapies, albeit less frequently.

The benefit of discussing the rationale of therapeutic interventions with perfectionist patients is that it normalizes the process for them. This can be important considering a proneness to feeling inadequate. If the therapeutic approach, for example, consists of working psychodynamically and discussing positive and negative transference, the process of free association can be beneficial. Teaching mindfulness skills (discussed in Chapter 6) and explaining the concept of the observing ego can also facilitate the patient's capacity for examining thought processes and emotional states in a less judgmental way.

The Observing Ego

The observing ego basically allows patients to monitor themselves and their actions as an uninvolved outsider. In explaining an observing ego to a patient, an example can be helpful, such as "Let's observe what happened with that interaction as though we were watching a character in a movie." This is a comment that patients can connect with, given the nontechnical language. It essentially encourages a slight detachment, creating for patients more distance and more freedom when discussing vulnerabilities. In addition, reframing the patient's ability to discuss emotions or anxiety as a psychological strength illustrating a well-developed observing ego can help facilitate the therapeutic alliance. As more genuine emotions are being discussed, patients ultimately feel connected to themselves and their therapist.

In addition to talking about therapy tasks, it is important to discuss therapy goals. This does not necessarily mean deciding on fixed goals but rather involves a dialogue about goals and expectations. Once goals are revealed, the therapist should communicate understanding of the goals discussed to the patient, which conveys an interest in understanding the patient and in the patient's well-being. This dialogue also clarifies potential misunderstandings.

Often, perfectionist patients do not initially have goals of being less perfectionistic. Several factors may account for this. Perfectionism is a trait rarely seen by the layperson as a conventional pathology, such as depression and anxiety. In addition, the trait may be seen as globally positive. Regardless of the reasons, introducing to patients the concept of looking at their perfectionism has beneficial psychological implications.

Discussing Perfectionism

A study conducted by Aldea, Rice, Gormley, and Rojas (2010) found that giving subjects education and feedback about adaptive and maladaptive perfectionism led to a reduction in a perfectionist subject's emotional reactivity and distress. There are several explanations as to why giving feedback about perfectionism can be helpful. First, by increasing awareness about perfectionism, patients can see the negative aspects of maladaptive perfectionism. They may be able to identify how their coping style may be affecting their career or social life. In addition, although patients do not explicitly express it, they may be aware that they have perfectionist traits that are problematic. According to self-verification theory, patients desire feedback, even negative feedback, if it conforms to their self-concept because it allows a sense of cohesion. Patients may feel understood when the therapist points out this personality component, which could lead to a stronger therapeutic alliance. They may also feel hope when they actively identify this personality trait as something that can be worked on.

As the study conducted by Aldea et al. (2010) indicates, giving feedback in a collaborative and interactive way about an individual's perfectionism is most effective. What follows is a brief transcript illustrating feedback related to perfectionism. The transcript is from a discussion with one of my patients who had been striving to obtain a promotion. She spent copious amounts of time at work reviewing documents to avoid any mistake. She also would take on as many projects as she could to earn positive feedback from her superiors. This patient has both socially and self-oriented perfectionism traits.

Dr. B: Being successful at work is extremely important to you.

Patient: Yes, I want to do well, and if I want to succeed I have to be perfect because it is very competitive. All it takes is one mistake and it's over.

Dr. B: Over?

Patient: That's right, over. I put myself at great risk for not getting the promotion.

Dr. B: So it sounds like you are walking on a tightrope. Tell me how that feels.

Patient: Stressful.

Dr. B: I can imagine. How do you deal with that stress?

Patient: I just keeping working harder to reach my goals.

Dr. B: So these goals keep you working hard, and to relieve stress you just work harder.

Patient: Yeah, that's right. [pause] I just don't see my friends that much because I am always working.

Dr. B: So trying to be perfect at work keeps you isolated socially.

Patient: I've always been the top in whatever I was doing. I was valedictorian; I was a state champion in track. No room for error.

Dr. B: So it sounds like the high expectations you have for yourself have been pervasive in a lot of areas of your life. What happens if you fall short of your expectations?

Patient: Total depression.

Dr. B: How bad does it get?

Patient: Well, not suicidal. I never attempted or had intentions or thoughts, but I get really hopeless.

Dr. B: Your high striving in some ways has been adaptive and helped you achieve goals. However, when you fall short, you really beat yourself up. You really punish yourself. What you are describing sounds like traits that resemble perfectionism. It sounds like you don't want to lower your standards and want to aim high, but there are consequences. What do you think?

Patient: There are consequences, but I don't want to lower my standards.

Dr. B: Well, maybe we can work on keeping your standards high but helping you relate differently to yourself when you fall short of meeting your standards.

Patient: That sounds good but hard to do. I do beat myself up; I always have.

Dr. B: It will take some time, but we will work on it.

As shown in this dialogue, I am acknowledging the adaptive aspects of the patient's perfectionism. At the same time, the dialogue illustrates the maladaptive aspects of her perfectionism in an interactive way. It sets the frame for working on her perfectionism and acknowledges it as a problem. Often I use the words *self-punishing* and *self-punitive* when giving feedback to patients who are self-castigating when they fall short of expectations. These words allow patients to feel they have permission to be more accepting of themselves.

Discussing the pros and cons of perfectionism with patients by focusing on the positive and negative aspects of their perfectionist coping style lays the groundwork for considering and motivating change. Patients are often reassured when given feedback that it may be adaptive to have high standards but that their reaction to not meeting their standards may be less adaptive. In a sense, they are not asked to give up their strivings but instead are asked to consider options aside from a punitive self-stance if their strivings do not become reality. Giving patients a new framework to understand and assess their perfectionism increases motivation for therapy, thus supporting the therapeutic alliance.

PERFECTIONISM AND SELF-ESTRANGEMENT

Many patients with perfectionism have covert therapy goals of asking the therapist to help them achieve their high perfectionist goals. For example, they enter therapy with the complaint that if they were a better wife or employee, they would be fine. They may be cut off and estranged from feelings and thoughts. The goals and what they are striving for may not be what they want unconsciously. As self-estrangement decreases, they can become more connected to themselves and to others. This allows the possibility of a strong therapeutic alliance.

Self-estrangement is a disconnection a person has with his or her thoughts, feelings, and behavior (Shapiro, 1999). People who are self-estranged are essentially influenced greatly by obligations or ideals of what they think they should do regarding their actions and behaviors. However, these supposed obligations or ideals run counter to their genuine feelings and thoughts. They may stem, for example, from internalized parental beliefs about right and wrong. Estranged individuals become so invested in these obligations that deviating from them creates intense anxiety. This anxiety may lead someone who is self-estranged to defend against awareness of thoughts and feelings that do not match his or her internalized obligations. In these individuals' speech, the therapist may hear self-estrangement when they feel someone is trying to convince them that their thoughts and ideas are in sync with their obligations.

Speech acts that are exaggerated or overemphasized are signs of self-estrangement (Shapiro, 1999). For example, consider a comment such as, "How can I still be dating that man? I get nothing from it." This is the person's attempt at self-deception. The person, unconsciously, is trying to convince herself that she doesn't have loving feelings toward her boyfriend. In this case, the woman feels obligated to hate the man because of her internalized ideals. She can't love a man whom she consciously perceives as treating her so poorly.

Socially oriented perfectionists are particularly prone to self-estrangement. A socially oriented perfectionist patient whom I refer to here as Allie often reported how much she liked to organize parties and events. She would do all the work for her upcoming events, with friends saying it must give her a great sense of satisfaction and confidence. Allie would get hyperinvolved when helping friends with chores or cumbersome and inconvenient tasks and would expect nothing in return. "I truly don't mind spending all the time and energy to help my friends," she said. In addition, she would frequently state, "There is just nothing more important in the world than my friends."

During one session, Allie realized she had forgotten a friend's birthday. She began to berate herself viciously and appeared to be crying at one point. When examining her closely, I realized the crying had a forced quality to it that made me feel less empathic toward her remarks. She seemed to be attempting to put on a sober expression. I continued to look at her confused and a bit perplexed. She responded by stating, "I do, however, get tired of always doing everything. It is damn tiring." The lack of empathy in my expression shifted Allie's awareness toward her estranged feelings and anger. I did not reinforce her attempt at her obligation to be angry. Often, when therapists see that someone is sad, they attempt to sympathize, which can support the patient's self-deception. When working with a perfectionist responding in an authentic fashion, not fusing with the patient's obligations can help expand his or her awareness as the patient reflects on the feedback given and as reevaluates his or her feelings. Self-oriented perfectionists also engage in self-deception regarding the importance of their personal goals. They may go on an exaggerated tirade about failing to fulfill important tasks or live up to ideals, and their reaction may seem artificial. Being made aware of the self-deception and of the estrangement process can help patients feel more genuinely connected to their emotions, as well as to the therapist supporting the alliance.

Although there are many techniques to help foster the therapeutic alliance, ruptures in the relationship are inevitable. The rest of this chapter and subsequent chapters discuss resolving therapy ruptures.

THERAPY RUPTURES

Ruptures are deteriorations in the quality of the relationship between patient and therapist. During a rupture, the patient may feel as though his or her needs are unmet. If ruptures occur and are not repaired, the alliance continues to deteriorate and the relationship declines.

Safran and Muran (2000) analyzed and developed a model for identifying and resolving ruptures. Their work discusses two distinct types of ruptures, referred to as withdrawal and confrontation ruptures. No formal research has been conducted to assess the association between type of rupture and perfectionist style. However, Safran and Muran's experiential observations indicate that withdrawal ruptures predominately reflect a socially oriented perfectionist style, whereas confrontation ruptures are characteristic of self- and other-oriented perfectionism. Individuals prone to withdrawal ruptures are highly concerned about connecting with others and are less likely to engage in outward conflict. They do not want to be seen negatively, similar to the sensitivity of socially oriented perfectionists. However, socially oriented perfectionists are hesitant to give direct and negative feedback because of the relationship ramifications. Conflict is thus expressed indirectly, if at all. Conversely, self- and other-oriented perfectionists are less concerned with relatedness. Establishing self-definition and identity are primary preoccupations. Thus, self- and other-oriented perfectionists are unlikely to refrain from expressing their thoughts and feelings assertively when they are involved in a conflict.

Withdrawal Ruptures

Safran and Muran's (2000) stage model to manage ruptures can be applied when working with the different perfectionist styles. To manage withdrawal ruptures, Safran and Muran suggest a stage model consisting of several steps:

1. Identifying the rupture
2. Disembedding the rupture
3. Making qualified assertions
4. Making self-assertions

These steps are explored in the sections that follow. Through them, the therapist and patient can achieve the overall goal of resolving ruptures: to help the patient feel comfortable being more self-assertive and become less preoccupied with fears about expressing negative thoughts and feelings toward others.

Rupture Identification

Withdrawal ruptures can be identified by denial of evident anger, short and terse responses, topic shifts, intellectualization, long-winded storytelling, and talking about irrelevant topics or other people. Comments such as, "I am somewhat frustrated with some comments you made last week, but it's not a big deal," reveal the quality of suppression therapists may see in withdrawal ruptures. These comments are called withdrawal markers. In the process of identifying the withdrawal marker, therapists may notice they are less attentive, working harder, or having difficulty keeping the patient's attention.

Disembedding the Rupture

The withdrawal of the patient may trigger the therapist to withdraw and vice versa. Comments that can begin the exploration of the process should focus on the here and now and should be curious and empathic. Comments such as the following can be beneficial and part of the disembedding process. This process consists of understanding what is happening interpersonally as the rupture is occurring.

"What are you experiencing?"
"I am not sure what is going on, but I think it may have something to do with the distant sound in your voice."
"What's going on for you right now?"
"I sense you are withdrawing."

The preceding comments are all plausible ways to begin the dialogue. In response to discussing the patient's withdrawal and making observations, the patient may intellectualize or discuss something abstractly, such as frustration with a friend, a boss, prior therapists, or the medical profession. In response, the therapist could benefit by redirecting the patient to the situation in the room, for example, saying, "I wonder if your frustration about . . . applies to me." Reassuring patients that it is not uncommon to talk negatively in a more general way when they are feeling frustrated with their therapist may also normalize the patients' experience.

Qualified Assertions

In the next phase of the process, patients may start to express some feelings about their thoughts and feelings but pull back on them. These mixed communication measures are referred to by Safran and Muran (2000) and by others as qualified assertions. A patient may say, "I am feeling a little disappointed, but it's not really anything significant," or may state, "I feel upset, but I know my feelings are illogical." Strategies to manage these types of qualified responses include exploring the different self-states. When undertaking this exploration, the therapist may communicate to the patient the following, "I hear that you have mixed feelings regarding this issue. On one hand, you feel your feelings are irrelevant. Conversely, you are disappointed. For a moment, if you are willing, let's put the feelings about being illogical aside and explore your disappointment."

Another technique is to provide the patient with feedback about his or her ambivalence, saying something like, "I sense that you start to express something and then you seem to pull back." In time, the therapist can explore the defense operation and the patient's hesitancy about expressing feelings directly. What does the patient risk by such expression—loss, abandonment, something else?

Self-Assertions

The process of exploring the patient's qualified assertions can lead to self-assertion, which consists of the patient expressing his or her needs directly. Often, helping socially oriented perfectionists express disappointment or negative feelings is a major treatment goal. This can help socially oriented perfectionists in their interpersonal relationships, thus decreasing distress.

Galena: Social Dissatisfaction

Galena was an executive who came to me for therapy because she had difficulty forming intimate relationships and was dissatisfied at work. She reported that in her relationships with men, she often found they left her precipitously, almost out of thin air, without warning. She also reported that she felt bosses at work took advantage of her. She reported working frequently on weekends and feeling like a slave. Her incapacity to navigate social and work environments left her feeling depressed and anxious. She often chose to acquiesce to others, which made her feel safe and secure but led to resentment and depression. She displayed traits that resembled socially oriented perfectionism.

After about a month of treatment, Galena reported that she was unsure of whether she would be reimbursed by her insurance company for the subsequent sessions and would have to look into it. She stated that if her insurance company was unable to cover the bulk of the sessions, she would have to put therapy on hiatus. The following week, after bringing up the finances of therapy, she stated that her insurance company would cover the therapy and that she could continue. She came in with a big smile on her face and appeared excited. "That is so great that my insurance will cover subsequent sessions. It's just terrific isn't it?" I felt detached and unmoved by her excitement and initially was unsure why. After reflecting on my withdrawn feelings, I got the impression that she was talking not to me but to herself. It was as though she was trying to convince herself that she was excited about therapy (self-estrangement). In addition, when discussing fees initially, she mentioned how she could manage the out-of-pocket costs regardless of what her insurance carrier reimbursed, so her comments did not feel genuine. I wondered whether in some way she had some ambivalent feelings about the therapy.

I told Galena that I noticed how she was expressing excitement about the therapy. I asked her to join in an experiment with me to imagine how she would have felt if she would not have been reimbursed and would have to forgo therapy. She reported that she would feel disappointed, but as she said this, I noticed a small smile flash across her face. I told her that I noticed she had smiled as she was talking. She stated, "Yes, I guess I would be disappointed, but at the same time relieved." I then pointed out that both sides of the feelings she was expressing were similar to a qualified assertion. I asked her for a moment to discuss the part of herself that would be relieved. She stated that at times she did not like coming to therapy. She said, "I just feel like, I talk and talk and I want more answers. I just want to feel better." This expression represented a self-assertion and was helpful in getting Galena to become less estranged from her direct feelings. With her feelings more directly expressed, how to meet her needs and improve the therapy relationship could be discussed directly.

Confrontation Ruptures

In contrast to socially oriented perfectionists, other-oriented perfectionists and self-oriented perfectionists (particularly those with other-oriented traits) tend to be less externally preoccupied with the opinions and beliefs of others. Consequently, expressing frustration tends to be less significant with these character styles. Other- and self-oriented perfectionists are likely to have confrontation ruptures in which anger about the therapeutic process may be expressed directly. Patients may directly indicate that they feel the therapist is incompetent. They may directly express irritation with the therapist or personal doubts about continuing. They may overtly complain about the lack of significant gains. Although self- and other-oriented perfectionists primarily engage in confrontation ruptures, they may also engage in withdrawal ruptures as guilty feelings emerge.

Self-oriented perfectionists (particularly those with other-oriented perfectionist traits) and other-oriented perfectionists engaging in confrontational styles may have underlying feelings of hopelessness and despair. Helping them to express the despair and fears of abandonment and vulnerability underneath their defensive posture of anger can often repair the rupture. Having a space where needs and feelings of hopelessness can be expressed directly can make them more connected to their vulnerable emotions—and subsequently more connected to their therapist and potentially to others whom they have alienated. When the patient can experience the therapist as a compassionate individual, he or she may in turn be able to develop more compassion toward himself or herself.

Similar to withdrawal ruptures, confrontation ruptures have a stage model (Safran & Muran, 2000):

1. Recognizing the rupture
2. Disembedding the rupture
3. Exploring the construal (the international matrix)
4. Expressing vulnerability

Recognizing the rupture, such as through confrontation markers, may be rather transparent due to the level of aggression that the patient may express toward the therapist. After noticing the confrontation rupture, discussing the dynamic that may be occurring between the therapist and the patient is the next step.

When therapists are confronted, they are likely to make interpretations or direct devaluing comments toward the patient. They may, for example, attribute the patient's aggression initially to intrapsychic dynamics or history, which places the responsibility on the patient. For example, a comment such as, "Your anger toward me seems familiar to the anger you have toward other authority figures in your life," suggests that the problem lies within the patient and disavows the patient's subjective experience. It also may be experienced as a counterattack.

A more mindful comment that begins the disembedding process may consist of noting to the patient that there appears to be a power struggle. This is an observation in which blame is not assigned. This comment, or meta-communication, suggests that the conflict is a process in which both parties are participating. Giving feedback to a patient about how he or she is affecting the therapist can also begin the process of ameliorating the patient's aggression and can help lead to the patient discussing his or her experience of the interaction.

When working with a patient to explore his or her interactional experience, the next step is to help the patient explore his or her experience. This again does not require interpretations of unconscious processes but rather explores the edge of awareness that may not be explicit. As the patient expresses personal experience and feelings, it is important that the patient's experience be validated. The therapist may also acknowledge his or her contribution to the dynamic or rupture. As therapists understand patients' subjective experiences in more nuanced ways, the therapists are less likely to act defensively. In many respects, understanding, empathizing, articulating, and exchanging subjective perspectives may constitute the final stage of the resolution process. Alternatively, patients may go deeper and explore their vulnerabilities.

During the process of exploring a patient's and a therapist's subjective experience, shifts often take place in which the patient may feel guilt regarding the expression of anger. The patient may minimize or discount feelings or may change the topic when approaching his or her anger. Conversely, when approaching sadness, the patient may move into an aggressive mode because the sadness may be too overwhelming. Monitoring these shifts and exploring with the patient when and why they occur may lead the patient to discover and express deeper feelings. This can lead, in turn, to the patient revealing his or her vulnerabilities.

Exploring vulnerabilities may take several months or even years. It can occur when the therapist has remained consistent and is willing to understand the patient's subjective experience and his or her own contribution to the dynamic, as well as when he or she is willing to contain the patient's aggression. When the patient is ready, the exploration of his or her vulnerability often provides a new experience in which underlying needs for nurturance are expressed. In many cases, the patient may express vulnerability with an emotional tone of despair, in contrast to an aggressive, sarcastic, or cynical tone that may push the therapist away.

Micah: Discussing Interaction

Micah was a 30-year-old man who came to therapy with problems regarding career and relationships. He had quit his job to discover his true passion. In the process of reviewing his career options, nothing ever met his standards. Although he would appear excited about a career option initially, he would shift into a devaluing mode and become dejected. His orientation toward his career mirrored his feelings toward other people, who also appeared to fall short of his expectations. His harsh expectations of others, as well as of himself, represented traits that coincide with other- and self-oriented perfectionism.

During our first visit, I noticed how uncomfortable his intense and unflinching stare made me. I had the feeling I was about to be reprimanded for something. One of his first comments to me was in regard to my office, which he referred to as "sparse." He stated that it made him wonder whether I was uptight or lacked creativity. Several sessions later, he commented on me not taking notes and explicitly questioned my competence (confrontation marker). I asked him how this made him feel and what it was like for him to be with a therapist whose competence he questioned. He responded by stating that it made him wonder whether he should continue. The dialogue regarding what occurred next is documented here.

Dr. B: So you may be asking yourself whether it makes sense to work together.

Patient: Exactly; I just don't think you can help me.

Dr. B: It's important you feel comfortable. I would like to help, and if I can't, I would like to find you someone who can.

Patient: Don't take it personally; I don't think anyone can help me. It's not you, I guess.

Dr. B: So it sounds like you feel hopeless.

Patient: I wouldn't say hopeless. I've just got to get focused, pull myself out of it, and take control.

Dr. B: Kind of like pull up your own bootstraps.

Patient: Yeah, I guess that's right. I've got to do it on my own. I mean, you can't help me. If you had any insights, it's not clear to me why you just don't come out with it already.

Dr. B: I kind of feel on the spot here and a bit anxious. I am unsure what to say.

Patient: Yeah, I guess in a way we are in the same boat. It's hopeless.

Dr. B: You also look sad when you say the word *hopeless*. There is sadness in your eyes that I haven't seen before.

Patient: I am sad and feel alone. I want help, I want to connect with something, and I just can't.

Dr. B: I can see that, and it's nice to hear you express your needs directly.

Strengthening the Therapeutic Alliance

In the preceding segment, the discussion was about the interaction. My capacity to stay with Micah's aggression and my self-disclosure had several positive effects. By allowing the patient to express his anger and by tolerating his anger, I was able to help the patient explore and communicate his vulnerability.

My self-disclosure about my anxiety to say anything served several purposes. First, it allowed me to express feelings without acting on them. Second, it showed Micah the type of effect his feelings were having on me. It also modeled for Micah how negative feelings can be expressed in a modulated fashion. Last, there was a parallel between what I was feeling—unable to perfectly meet expectations—and what Micah feels chronically. When I articulated this to Micah, he felt that I was trying to understand him and in some ways did understand him. My effort increased the trust between us and allowed Micah to venture into discussing some of his vulnerabilities.

As seen here, Safran and Muran (2000) provide one model for dealing with ruptures. As shown throughout the rest of the chapters, there are other models and ways of dealing with therapy ruptures that are influenced by the theoretical perspective the therapist is using to understand the patient.

THREE

Interpersonal Approach and Perfectionists

A good garden may have some weeds.

—Thomas Fuller

This chapter gives a brief overview of interpersonal psychotherapy and how it applies to perfectionist patients. Three cases of patients with perfectionist traits are discussed. Examples of techniques used to help these patients are described. In the last section, communication techniques and strategies to use with perfectionist patients are clearly outlined.

BASIC PRINCIPLES: BEHAVIOR AND PATHOLOGY

From an interpersonal perspective, individuals are viewed as social beings who are shaped by relationships and can be understood only by observing how they function in relationships (Sullivan, 1953). Interpersonal theory states that people have two major needs that operate within an interpersonal context: needs for satisfaction and needs for security. Satisfaction needs are classified as needs for emotional contact, self-expression, and tenderness. These needs develop in a complex fashion throughout the human life span. A person's security needs relate to avoiding anxiety and are more dominant than a person's needs for satisfaction (Greenberg & Mitchell, 1983; Sullivan, 1953). Avoiding anxiety is the primary motivating factor that guides behavior when a person interacts with others (Mitchell & Black, 1996).

According to interpersonal theory, anxiety is contagious. For instance, a mother's or caretaker's anxiety can make a child anxious, and a child's anxiety can trigger a parent's anxiety. Through empathic linkage, the child is able to distinguish between the anxious and the nonanxious states of his caretaker or mother (Greenberg & Mitchell, 1983). Early on, the child learns that certain behaviors generate the tenderness and nonanxious states expressed by his or her mother. Sullivan (1953) classifies the child's behavior that induces tenderness in the mother as the "good me." The child's behavior that induces anxiety is associated with the "bad me" and "not me" (Sullivan, 1953). As a child develops, so does his or her self-system, which contains security operations designed to avoid anxiety or behaviors associated with anxiety (bad me or not me). One such security operation is selective attention, in which a person may not attend to relevant information and instead focuses only on certain aspects of an interaction with another person to avoid anxiety (Greenberg & Mitchell, 1983; Sullivan, 1953).

The level of pathology an individual may struggle with is related to the level of anxiety that person experiences or experienced in his or her family environment. A person who has grown up in an environment with extensive anxiety has a limited range of interpersonal behaviors associated with the good me (i.e., behavior that is not associated with parental anxiety).

Engaging in interpersonal behavior associated with a parent's anxiety is frightening to a child, and doing so can make the child feel as an adult that he or she will lose contact with others, which is equivalent to a loss of one's sense of self (Mitchell, 1988). In essence, to avoid anxiety, the person is left with a restricted interpersonal style or behavior limiting his or her capacity to connect with others and achieve satisfaction. The person may perceive others in current relationships similar to how he or she perceived previous caretakers and may continue to respond with restricted interpersonal behaviors. Consequently, an individual's rigid interpersonal style may induce others to behave in a manner that may perpetuate maladaptive and repetitive patterns, further interfering with that person's satisfaction (Mitchell, 1988).

For example, a client's mother became consistently anxious when the client was sad and tearful. As a result, while growing up, the client's expression of negative affect was associated with the "bad me." The client may have expected and perceived that people besides her mother will also experience her sadness as anxiety provoking; thus, she squelched negative or sad affective experiences when interacting with others. In response to her lack of expression of sad affect, others may have felt as though she doesn't need support and thus did not provide it, leaving the client feeling unsatisfied. Her experience of others as unsupportive reinforced her expectations, beliefs, and rigid interpersonal style.

TREATMENT AND BEHAVIORAL CHANGE

In therapy, the client and therapist engage in interpersonal exchanges that mirror client interactions with others in his or her external world. The client responds to and perceives the therapist in a fashion similar to the way he or she perceived significant others during childhood and throughout life. According to contemporary interpersonal theorists, the client is not necessarily projecting distorted images of significant others onto the therapist (a more traditional or psychoanalytic view of transference). Rather, the client may be accurately, albeit selectively, attending to behavior by the therapist that confirms expectations that the therapist is similar to others in the client's life or past (e.g., parents)

(Mitchell, 1988; Mitchell & Black, 1996). The client's transference is viewed not as faulty displacement but rather as a limited and narrow perspective stemming from significant childhood and ongoing experiences that shape how the client organizes, perceives, and responds to the therapist and others. In addition, the client's restricted interpersonal or narrow style and defenses against anxiety often induce the therapist to reenact familiar roles that the client experiences with others (Levenson, 1983; Mitchell, 1988).

The therapist's role is to help the client expand and develop more flexible, more variegated, and less restricted ways of interacting and connecting with others (Mitchell, 1988). The therapist helps the client accomplish this goal via inquiry or by working collaboratively with the client to understand and develop insight about his or her interpersonal style and how this style may perpetuate his or her difficulties (Mitchell, 1988; Mitchell & Black, 1996; Sullivan, 1953). The therapist explores with the client questions such as the following: Who says what in interactions? When do you notice anxiety in interpersonal relationships? How do you manage your anxiety? How does your interpersonal style influence others? What is gained by engaging others interpersonally in this fashion? What is lost? What are your expectations of others? In addition, the therapist and client work to understand the etiology of how his or her interpersonal style developed.

As mentioned, therapists unwittingly finds themselves in relationship scenarios similar to those that the client experiences with others. The therapist needs to be attuned to the client's transference, countertransference, and what is happening in the therapy relationship (the here and now) (Levenson, 1983; Mitchell, 1988). The therapist in essence is asking him- or herself, and possibly the client, what is going on between us in this therapy rupture? (see Chapter 2). The therapist, for example, amid a sadomasochistic dynamic with the client, may explore with the client how they got into the situation. They exchange subjective experiences (transference and countertransference experiences) and discuss new ways of relating that may be more authentic for the therapist and more satisfying for the client.

The therapist also helps the client make links between parallels that occur in the client's outside relationships and in the current therapy relationship. Their discussion about the current relationship and their exchange of different subjective experiences can encourage the client to experiment with new ways of interacting. In a sense, talking about the interaction can be viewed as a new experience for the client. Having a new experience, or undergoing experiential learning, is highly mutative from an interpersonal perspective. The client's capacity to have a new relationship experience can extend to his or her outside world, leading to an expanded interpersonal repertoire (Mitchell, 1988; Mitchell & Black, 1996).

The repetitive dynamics that induce the therapist to taking on a specific interpersonal role or emotional experience are referred to as enactments. Not all enactments that occur in the therapy relationship directly parallel the relationship role the client experiences in other relationships. The dynamic that emerges between the client and the therapist may be idiosyncratic to their interaction.

Enactments may also communicate how a client is treated by others rather than how that person relates to others. A client who is often submissive when interacting with others may act dominant when interacting with the therapist. This communicates to the therapist what the client experienced with others who may have been domineering. The therapist may even feel similar emotions and psychological processes through this interaction that the client feels in his or her intrapsychic world.

THERAPEUTIC ACTION WITH THE SOCIALLY ORIENTED PERFECTIONIST

Interpersonal psychotherapy can be particularly beneficial for individuals with socially oriented perfectionism. These people, as discussed in earlier chapters, believe that others have excessively high expectations. If they fail to meet other people's expectations, they expect that they will be rejected, devalued, and possibly even abandoned. Socially oriented perfectionists often desire to avoid rejection and abandonment at all costs. At the same time, they often desire a connection with other people. Consequently, these individuals may mask true feelings, thoughts, or needs to maintain relationship stability. Teaching perfectionists new ways of interacting, ways in which they learn to be less preoccupied with being perfect in their relationships, can be beneficial and mutative.

Frank: The Secret

Frank is a gay male who came in for treatment after moving from Florida to New York City. He sought treatment because he felt isolated and found that he was unable to connect with other people and make new friends. He was often preoccupied with rejection. He believed overall that men would find him unattractive and women would find him boring and uninteresting. In relationships, he found he was reluctant to share opinions and thoughts, particularly if he felt they differed from those of his peers. Frank presented as bubbly and agreeable, and he always had a bright smile. He vigorously watched all popular television shows and read both liberal and conservative papers so that he could fit into and flow with conversations. He wanted to give people the impression that he was smart and full of energy.

In therapy sessions, quiet and long silences were common. Frank often gave the appearance that everything was okay. He would flash a bright smile, followed by an anxious laugh, and say that he was "fine." I found that I would ask, more than usual, a great number of questions to fill the silences with content. At one point, I suggested that he keep a diary and bring it in so that I could help him identify thoughts and feelings. He agreed, and every week he would send me pages and pages of thoughts, feelings, and observations. This provided insight into what was going on in his world, and we were able to make some links among interpersonal style, family dynamics, and vivid dream life.

Frank's diaries would often consist of vivid dreams about being chased or drowning. We were able to link how these images seemed to coincide with his feeling that he lacked a voice in his interaction with others. He began to reveal how peer rejection and self-image played roles in shaping his accommodating and inhibited interpersonal style. He told me that as a child he could not turn to his family because expressing negative affect was strongly discouraged. He expressed terror regarding rejection from his family because of his sexual orientation. He often complimented the therapy and my ability to understand him. Despite this new therapeutic material, I felt our dynamic in the therapy sessions did not change much. I was still doing a lot of work making connections and inferences, and sharing my own associations. I also found it striking that his writing, which was emotionally charged and displayed nuanced emotional understanding, did not match his detached and indifferent presentation, which was most pronounced in our sessions.

When asked about the therapeutic process and what it was like to be in the room with me, he expressed that he felt as though he was a burden. He reported that he often felt guilty about expressing his problems, because he viewed them as insignificant and felt as though my time would better spent listening to someone who had "real issues." He imagined that I was bored and did not look forward to seeing him. Ironically, I did not see him as a burden but rather felt that he may perceive me in that fashion. I felt intrusive and that I was taking up too much space. I felt, similar to his dreams, that I may have been suffocating him. He was intrigued by this disclosure but denied that he felt suffocated by me or that he experienced me as intrusive. He reported that he liked my level of activity. We talked about how our participation and current way of working felt safe for both of us. He could be less revealing as I took up more room. By consistently filling the therapy space with my thoughts and ideas, it was making him less anxious. I asked

Frank how he would feel if I experimented with being quieter. He reported that he thought this might make him more uncomfortable because when there were silences, he would become anxious and wonder what I might be thinking about. I validated his feelings of anxiety and told him to spontaneously reveal his worries and concerns when they came up. I also told him that although I felt his writing was helpful for the therapeutic process, he should, for a brief time, refrain from bringing it to the therapy sessions. He agreed with this plan, and in the following sessions I tried to resist the pull to fill conversational space in the therapy room.

During one of our sessions, Frank looked at me after a long silence and started laughing. I asked him to tell me what he was thinking. He told me he thought I was looking at him funny. I asked him what he thought I was thinking. He told me I was probably thinking about how weird he was and about how I was wasting my time. I reassured him that I did not feel that way. He then revealed that he thought I was probably looking at him and thinking about how unintelligent he was. I told him that was not the case and wondered whether he felt people in general thought that often. He reported that he did and began to cry.

I asked Frank about his tears, and he began to tell me that he wanted to talk to me about a secret he had been hiding for a long time. I responded that he was welcome to tell me but did not have to until he felt comfortable. He stated that he wanted to tell me and began to report that he had been sexually abused by his brother yet had told no one, even in his family. He stated that he had to put on happy face and act as though everything was okay but that he was filled with anger. He felt he had to put on a show for his family. He felt that if he spoke about his feelings and what happened, his family would not believe him and he would be abandoned. In essence, he felt suffocated by holding onto this secret. To this day, he cringes at family gatherings and at how his parents coddle and take care of his older brother, who he sees as a helpless victimizer.

Similar to his family interactions, he learned to interact with people by withholding his thoughts and feelings, fearing that revealing himself would lead to abandonment. He felt he had to be perfect and live up to the expectations of others. Negative affect would disrupt this perfect bubble he felt he had to portray.

These new data provided us with a great deal of insight into Frank's interpersonal style. In our therapy relationship, we were able to have a new experience in which he was able to reveal himself without being abandoned. The new experience eventually expanded his interpersonal repertoire.

MIXED TRAITS OF SOCIALLY AND SELF-ORIENTED PERFECTIONISM

Patients often have traits that are consistent with both socially oriented perfectionism and self-oriented perfectionism. These patients may be concerned with the perceptions that others have of them, in addition to having intense concerns regarding success. On the surface, these patients may not display a concern with others' views. Others may perceive them as aloof or indifferent. However, these patients may be highly concerned with their social perception by others, as well as with their personal achievements.

Denise: Defined by Success

Denise, a patient of mine, exhibited both socially oriented and self-oriented perfectionism. Denise never knew her father and had little contact with her mother, who gave birth to her at the age of 16. For many years while growing up, Denise moved around a great deal. She lived with her grandmother and an uncle, and at the age of 10 she moved in with her aunt and three cousins. She felt unwanted in general as a child, particularly when living with her aunt. She reported that often her aunt and uncle would go away on trips, leaving her behind with a babysitter. She reported a vivid memory in which her aunt gave her a dress on her birthday. She wore it with great pride but then overheard her cousins talking about the gift. She stated that she heard them whispering about how inappropriate it was for their mother to give Denise a gift considering that she was not and would never be a part of the family. Denise was devastated. She reported that the disappointment with the family and feelings of abandonment led her to become avoidant of others. She became preoccupied with achievement in all realms academically and in employment situations. She defined herself by how many sales she made at work and her upward mobility. She projected the image that nothing mattered but her achievement of career goals.

Initially, Denise came to therapy because she was in a marriage that she desired to end. Feeling like a failure for not having a successful marriage was the most difficult emotion for her to tolerate. The shame of not being successful and not living up to her personal self-view and goal was crushing and, for her, led to depression. She also struggled with work issues. Despite excellent feedback and success at work, she felt as though she was not doing well enough. She would berate herself profusely for any mistake she made at work. The major therapeutic action consisted of two components: my nonpunitive demeanor and the intimacy that eventually developed in the therapy relationship.

During our work together, Denise offered little material spontaneously. However, she was not shy about communicating her desire to be independent. In time, she displayed good insight and was able to link her history of family disappointment and her reluctance to depend on others. She feared that like her aunt and uncle, others would leave her. She playfully informed me that she wasn't going to report explicitly what was on her mind because she did not want to depend on me. I believed that by making this comment, Denise was suggesting, "I don't depend on people, but I want to try to depend on you." When I told her my interpretation, she smiled but would not endorse it with a conventional "yes." She revealed how depending on others meant she needed others and was not self-sufficient or competent. This thought pattern and the related behavior are indicative of self-oriented perfectionism. In addition, she feared being rejected by others and thus avoided intimacy to prevent this from occurring, tapping into her socially oriented perfectionist traits.

After making some progress during our work together, Denise began to miss sessions. Initially, she blamed her hectic schedule. After pointing out that I had noticed she had missed therapy only after an emotional session in which she began to open up more, she said emotional sessions made her feel like a failure and that she was weak. This is not uncommon for perfectionist patients. After talking about her life, she would replay all her weaknesses and end up judging herself more after the session, increasing negative emotions. Her punitive stance toward herself was a dynamic that was germane to her problems and occurred in many contexts. In addition, her missed sessions were related to fears regarding her intimacy with me. As she started to share her feelings, she felt closer to me and was fearful that she may depend on me too greatly. She then feared that I would leave her. To avoid this rejection, she avoided me. Although her interpersonal protection and avoidance of others made her feel safe, it pushed people away.

I shared with Denise how I felt distant from her when she disappeared. She was able to see that she may have been pushing away other people in her life by perpetuating a similar dynamic. Although I still felt distance from Denise at times, my overall consistent availability and desire to stay with her in the therapeutic alliance helped debunk previous beliefs about what would happen if she became close to someone. She learned through our therapy relationship that intimacy was not necessarily associated with abandonment.

What was most helpful to Denise about our interaction was the straightforward stance I took toward the missed sessions. Keeping in mind how punitive she is toward herself and toward her behaviors that she perceives may be mistakes, I made an extra effort to manage my response to her missed sessions in a matter-of-fact way. This does not mean I was disingenuous or masking anger; rather, I consciously conveyed understanding and compassion when talking about the missed sessions. My accepting and nonjudgmental position in general helped her model a kinder, gentler approach to managing mistakes. I believe that in our therapy work together Denise became able to internalize a less harsh stance toward herself.

Amy: Always the Confidant

Amy's Anger

Amy, a 50-year-old female, has traits falling within the socially oriented perfectionist range. Her mother and father often became involved in altercations of high intensity. The content of her parent's arguments usually revolved around financial issues. Amy's mother was frequently put under a microscope. Although she mostly spent wisely, if she bought herself new clothes or purchased food that seemed pricey, a loud verbal altercation ensued. Amy's mother also wanted to pursue her passion to study art, but her husband felt that this was a waste of time. Amy's father was extremely withholding and physically abusive. If he was displeased with dinner or if anything went wrong, he blamed Amy's mother. Altercations often escalated rapidly into physical violence over a minor frustration that her father had. Amy's mother wanted to leave her father but felt unable to do so because of financial dependence.

The daughter became her mother's confidant. Amy, in a sense, was her mother's emotional caretaker. She listened empathically to her mother's worries and concerns and always made herself available to be supportive. Amy did not go to college as she wanted to so that she could be close to her mother. While growing up, Amy did not discuss her own problems with her mother. She feared that sharing problems with boyfriends and issues of getting picked on at school would destabilize her relationship with her mom. Affirmation, acceptance, and connection would be established only by being the trouble-free caretaker.

Amy grew up in Ohio, and she desperately wanted a life different from that of her mother. She moved to New York City for the opportunities that she dreamed may be available. For 6 months, she dated a man who promised her what she deemed as a life of possibility. However, as time progressed, Amy's hopes and dreams faded and felt unrealistic. She often expressed her life as consisting of few viable options. Once married, Amy felt as though she lived in a prison, trapped with a man whom she referred to as narcissistic, and she was terrifically unhappy. She felt suffocated by her husband, who she described as financially successful and creative but who needed constant reassurance. Her husband talked incessantly about his work concerns. He obsessed about whether clients would like his proposals and consistently felt he was not good enough—despite promotions, awards, and positive feedback from colleagues. Amy received multiple daily emails from her husband and had numerous conversations with him regarding his self-doubts. Conversely, her husband was absent regarding Amy's emotional and career needs. Amy always wanted to go to college and looked into taking some evening courses. Her husband, however, refused to pay for a course to help her achieve this goal. He told her that they could not afford it financially, which Amy stated in her therapy sessions was not the case. According to Amy, her husband believed she did not need to obtain an education because she was going to stay at home and did not need to work.

Socially, Amy described her husband as lifeless, often refusing to go out with others. When they did go out, she reported that he was preoccupied with his shortcomings and did not engage. Amy stated that when they went out by themselves for her birthday or Valentine's Day, the conversation always focused on her husband.

In our therapy sessions, Amy revealed that she was afraid of leaving her husband because she feared that she could not support herself without him. She did not want to give up the New York City lifestyle to which she had become accustomed. She also did not want to return home to Ohio. She reported that she grew up in a small town, where divorce would be viewed by others as a failure, and that she would feel deeply shamed. Her plan was to become licensed as a nurse and thus become independent financially and emotionally. Although this was her plan, she worried greatly about whether she would be able to go through with it. How could she carve out study time if she was always at the beck and call of her husband?

Amy and the Enactment

Amy often found that in interpersonal dynamics, there is one giver and one taker. In her relationship with her husband, she is emotionally available at all times. In contrast, her husband is the taker whose needs are always prominent. The giver-and-taker dynamic is prevalent in Amy's interactions with friends and family. In our therapy relationship, I believed the same dynamic was developing, except that the roles were reversed: I was in the giving position and felt stuck.

During one session, Amy expressed that she felt that I was withholding and was not saying everything on my mind. She was correct. I validated her perceptions and disclosed my experience. I told Amy that at times I refrained from sharing my thoughts and often debated the best course of action in my head. I told her that I held back feelings and thoughts because I anticipated that she would perceive my comments as unhelpful. As a result, I often felt invisible in our interactions. My tone while expressing this was of a curious nature, attempting to illustrate a "wondering out loud" position. I wanted to convey an invitation to Amy to explore why this was happening. I wanted to illustrate that I was open to her influence.

Amy initially was frustrated with my response. She started to yell at me and called me clueless and unable to express myself. After several minutes of this type of criticism and hesitation, she began to cry and revealed that she identified with my lack of voice and feeling invisible. She made the connection that this is how she feels in her marriage. We talked about how things could be different in the therapy relationship. I encouraged her to continue to share her experience of me. She encouraged me to express my opinions more, even though it would be difficult for her if they differed from what she wanted to hear. We talked about how we would both commit ourselves to the therapy relationship and continue with it even if we were angry.

I believe that on a nonconscious level, Amy was communicating about our relationship via enactment, essentially saying, "Dr. Brustein, this is what I have to deal with. Show me a new way out." By disclosing my countertransference experience, I modeled how she could express herself in a way other than accommodation. As a result, Amy was able to have a new experience in which both parties could share thoughts and feelings and survive. In a sense, we were both giving and taking, and our exchange had reciprocity. This differs greatly from her other relationships. As time went on, Amy was able to transfer what she learned in our relationship to her relationships with others. She began to speak more openly to her husband and express what she needed. She began to set boundaries and ask for more space. She felt more confident in herself as she learned to stand up for what she wanted. She in essence became less preoccupied with others' perception of her and trusted that relationships could survive even if she was not fully accommodating to another's wants and needs. This is the dynamic that many socially oriented perfectionists struggle with. Showing and modeling for them new ways of interacting can be greatly helpful.

ATTRIBUTIONAL INTERPRETATIONS AND COMMENTS

In addition to the enactment that took place in the preceding therapy relationship, the client was able to develop a new interpersonal style, which was facilitated by attributional comments (Wachtel, 2008). This use of attributional comments came up when I worked with Amy on how to manage her relationship with her husband. When asked about what she would risk if she discussed her feelings with her husband, Amy would smirk and say, "That won't work." Other questions regarding alternative interpersonal strategies were met with the same resistance. Interpretations such as "You feel the only way to relate to your husband is to be compliant, similar to how you related with your mother" also were dismissed. The problem with my initial approach was that it created an adversarial dynamic. In essence, my comments communicated that I was trying to persuade Amy into doing something different. I may also have been conveying to her that I knew something that she did not. When working with Amy, who has perfectionist traits, conveying that I had knowledge she did not could induce shame and vulnerability. She could not play the role of knowing caretaker. This created anxiety and contradicted core aspects of what she felt she needed to do to relate with others.

Consequently, I adapted my approach and began to make comments such as, "You are so giving to your husband and you want more. You feel suffocated, and that seems natural given the circumstances. This issue has been going on for a long time. Even though a large part of you feels like it seems like an impossible task, you are looking for a new way to relate to him and get your voice to be heard." This attributed to the patient knowledge of other ways to manage her interpersonal dynamic, rather than me, as her therapist, telling her that this is the case. The comments conveyed that Amy was already actively looking for a new way of engaging and relating. Thus, I was not telling her what she should be doing but rather acknowledging what she was already aware of and beginning to do.

Wachtel (2008) refers to these types of comments as attributional interpretations. Attributional interpretations are designed to manage defenses and resistance that patients may exhibit when receiving feedback about behavior. Attributional comments convey to patients that they have insight regarding behavior or an interpersonal style that may be conflictual. The stance of the therapist when making attributional comments is not of bringing news or interpretations that are out of patients' awareness. Rather, the therapist couches comments, suggesting that the patient on some level may be aware of the problematic aspects of behavior in which he or she is engaging. This technique is crucial for patients with perfectionistic tendencies.

When making attributional comments, it is important to not make unfounded comments that do not match the patient's experience or emerging thoughts and feelings. For example, Amy was clearly frustrated with her husband. The first part of my comment validated this experience. The second part of my comment, regarding her desire to look for a new way of relating, was grounded in her experience by her frustration with her current state of affairs. Amy was tired of giving in to others. She stated that she had no time for herself and needed more space to study and live her life. She wanted something new.

Attributional comments thus focus on or attend to data regarding what the patient is doing productively or is on the verge of or thinking about doing, to push the patient forward (Wachtel, 2008). Overall, the attributional comments and interpretations I made to Amy helped her form a collaboration or agreement in which we worked together on ways in which she could expand her interpersonal repertoire beyond the caretaker role.

COMMUNICATION STRATEGIES

The clinical exchanges in this chapter illustrate several examples of important components and types of communication to consider when working through enactments and resistance with perfectionist patients. Some communication strategies, such as attributional comments, are helpful in working through resistance that perfectionist patients may exhibit. The following pages review the strategies I used with the patients described in this chapter, as well as other points and strategies to consider when working with perfectionist patients.

1. *Validating the patient's perception of the therapist's countertransference.* When a patient accurately perceives the therapist's countertransference, one inclination may be to explore why the patient is thinking or feeling that way. A line of inquiry such as, "What makes you think that?" or "Have you ever thought that before about me?" may enhance the therapist's understanding of the patient's transference reactions. However, the perfectionist patient, who can be hypersensitive to judgment, may assume that by asking questions rather than making an acknowledgment, the therapist implies that his or her observations are a distortion or a displaced projection. This may lead to further resistance. When working with Amy, validating her perception that I was "holding back" helped her open up more about her thoughts and feelings and initiated a meta-communication dialogue.

    In addition, if therapists can acknowledge an emotional state, particularly a negative one, this may act as an adaptive modeling experience. For example, if a patient notices the therapist is not paying diligent attention, and the therapist believes this observation is accurate, acknowledging it can be valuable. In a sense, the therapist can show the patient that imperfections can be tolerated, which may help the patient internalize a similar stance toward his or her own flaws or imperfections.

2. *Offering a therapeutic demeanor and stance.* When working with perfectionist patients, many countertransference reactions may take place, leading to disengagement or an inflated sense of power. Patients who are perfectionists with dismissive traits, like Denise, act as though they do not need others. This can

cause the therapist to remain unengaged or become frustrated, pushing the therapist from his or her stance. Awareness of what is potentially being replayed can help the therapist remain engaged and discuss the dynamic with the patient. Maintaining an engaged attitude can be helpful with a perfectionist like Denise, who expects rejection.

Conversely, a perfectionist patient like Amy, who is prone to pleasing others, can be gratifying for a therapist. Basking in affirmation, the therapist may be pushed into acting like an all-knowing guru while the patient takes on a passive and eager student role. Perpetuating this dynamic can ultimately leave the patient feeling a lack of efficacy or as though the patient is unable to express him- or herself, the way he or she may feel in other relationships. To a certain extent, this dynamic between therapist and patient may be inevitable; however, it is important to find a way to work out of the dynamic into a new, progressive one.

3. *Jumping to conclusions.* In discussing and working through enactments with patients with perfectionism, it is important to explore and communicate without jumping to conclusions that may foreclose future exploration. Therapists should start with an observation about the patient, rather than first disclosing feelings or how the patient is making them feel. For example, a comment such as "I feel you're more distant, and I was wondering if this has to do with anything regarding our last session" may exacerbate the patient's defensiveness. The comment assumes that the patient is feeling more distant and consequently reacting to the therapist in a removed fashion. The more adaptive comment may be the question, "Are you feeling more distant?" Following up with more questions to get the patient to reflect on why he or she may be feeling more distant would be appropriate once the initial observation has been accepted.

4. *Allowing communication transparency.* Communication transparency consists of letting the patient know the rationale for poising

certain questions, interpretations, or interventions. Letting the patient understand the purpose of therapeutic actions can decrease resistance. When working with Frank, discussing experimenting with silence and the reason for the experiment helped him express fears and concerns about trying something new. This consequently helped him create a safe place that allowed him to take the next step.

Wondering aloud also helps transparency. The technique consists of suggesting an idea that the therapist has about the patient and inviting the patient to correct, modify, or disavow the therapist's thoughts. For example, a therapist may say to a patient, "I am not sure what to make of your tendency to date women who are unavailable, but I was thinking it may in some way be safe for you. I was wondering if this resonates with you in any way or what you think about this idea." Inviting the patient to participate in the creation of an idea or hypothesis can help the patient feel more comfortable accepting feedback. This technique gives explicit permission for the patient to correct the therapist—and to think about the therapist's idea.

5. *Joining.* This technique was implemented with Frank and consists of temporarily merging and perpetuating a defense or style that the patient feels comfortable engaging in but that ultimately may be problematic. Initially, I was taking up a lot of space with questions, which was perpetuating Frank's tendency to avoid and refrain from expressing emotions. In addition, writing assignments allowed Frank to distance himself from communicating his feelings face to face. My joining with Frank may have been elicited by my anxiety about making him anxious. In essence, with Frank, I believed that experimenting with silence prior to establishing a strong alliance may have been problematic. Such long-term joining would likely not lead to therapeutic change. However, for a short amount of time, joining may help create an initial bond, and it may form the prerequisite safety

that an individual with perfectionistic tendencies may need before he or she can risk making him- or herself more vulnerable.

6. *Showing nonverbal awareness and communication.* Extensive research illustrates that when observing nonverbal behavior or emotions of another person, mirror neurons are triggered. This creates a simultaneous pattern of neural activity in the observer's right hemisphere that coincides with the person being observed. When working with a perfectionist patient, the therapist may gain insight into the patient's feelings or emotional states by paying attention to his or her own feelings. Perfectionist patients often are reluctant to reveal aspects about themselves or self-disclose. They may exhibit nonverbal behavior, which elicits emotions within the therapist. It can be beneficial to be aware of these emotions, because they may mirror the patient's feelings. As therapists, paying attention to our own anxiety can help us understand when the patient is anxious, as well as what makes the patient anxious. In addition, by being aware of our nonverbal behavior and what it communicates, we can help a patient feel more comfortable or relaxed. For example, a perfectionist patient who has difficulty discussing his or her feelings may calm down by observing the therapist taking a deep breath.

7. *Providing metaphors.* Using metaphors or stories can help patients with perfectionist traits receive feedback in a less defensive way and can mitigate resistance. When working with some patients, I refer to a story or character that may resemble the patient. Talking about the character or story can help the patient analyze his or her issues in a more removed way, because the patient is in essence talking not only about him- or herself but also about a similar character (see the section on the observing ego in Chapter 2). When working with Amy, I recall thinking about the Shel Silverstein children's story titled *The Giving Tree*. The story in essence captures the theme of the socially oriented perfectionist. In the story, the tree has a relationship with a boy

in which the tree gives the boy everything it has: from shade, to its apples, to its branches. The tree gives so much to the boy that the tree ends up with nothing left but a stump. I used this story to help Amy understand her interpersonal style. It seemed that this was helpful, and it led her to look at herself more deeply. She made some points, stating that the tree was happy in the end. I asked whether she felt that living like the tree would be fulfilling to her. Using the story as a technique helped Amy assess the pros and cons of her interpersonal style, leading her to reconsider it.

FOUR

Self-Psychology and Perfectionism: Consolidation of One's Sense of Self

If people reach perfection they vanish, you know.

—T. H. White, *The Once and Future King*

Self-psychology aptly describes the psychological issues and dynamics of patients with perfectionism. In this chapter, self-psychological theory and techniques and ways in which self-psychology can be helpful when treating perfectionist patients are described.

SELF-PSYCHOLOGY THEORY AND DEVELOPMENT

Self-psychology, a theory developed by Heinz Kohut (1971), views pathology as stemming from unmet developmental needs. Kohut classified developmental, or self-object, needs into three categories: mirroring, idealizing, and twinship. When these needs are neglected, development is stunted or arrested.

Needs for affirmation or validation are referred to as mirroring needs (Kohut, 1971). These needs help people feel confident and valued. People want their accomplishments, thoughts, and feelings to be affirmed. When this occurs, adequate self-esteem and confidence develop.

Appropriate parental mirroring responses to a child include validating the child's fantasies and positive attributes. For example, suppose a 4-year-old child is wearing a Superman cape around the house and pretending he is saving the planet. The phase-appropriate mirroring response from a parent is a comment validating the child's fantasy, such as "Good job, Superman." Over time, these types of mirroring responses to the child's exhibitionism and grandiosity give him stable self-esteem and self-validation. His parents may gradually channel these affirmations in realistic directions as the child grows older. Consequently, a child with adequate self-mirroring responses develops a cohesive sense around this realm of development. He internally develops positive feelings and can sustain his sense of self even when approbation and approval are not forthcoming.

Idealizing needs (Kohut, 1971) refer to the need to have strong figures, parents, or caretakers to look up to and admire. When these needs are met, an individual feels a sense of safety in the world and is able to develop realistic goals. Phase-appropriate idealizing responses to children may consist of parents feeling comfortable with children who ask about their work or endeavors. For instance, a child may ask her father what he did during the day. An age-appropriate response may be for the father to describe his tasks. A deleterious response may be to shy away from the child's curiosity by avoiding the question or saying, "Oh, nothing important."

Children look to their parents to be strong and powerful. A child with a strong image of his or her parents or caretakers can bask in their glory. These adults are thus seen as having the strength to help the child manage and navigate the world. The child slowly learns the parents' imperfections, is able to see them in a realistic way, and in turn develops realistic goals and ideals.

Twinship needs (Kohut, 1984) refer to needs regarding affiliation with someone or something. More specifically, twinship needs consist of a person being on the same level as others and seeing himself or herself as similar to a group or person. Respecting the autonomy of children, and the unique attributes they bring to situations, can help satisfy twinship needs.

Although all self-object needs arise in childhood, people continue to require a certain level of fulfillment of these needs from others throughout their lifetime. Overall, the major self-psychological therapeutic action discussed later in this chapter is to provide for developmental needs that are stunted or arrested.

SELF-PSYCHOLOGY AND PATHOLOGY

As mentioned earlier, pathology develops when self-object needs are not met by caretakers. An individual's pathology can vary depending upon which needs are neglected.

An individual with unmet mirroring needs may greatly require validation. In many cases, mirroring needs become problems for perfectionist patients because these needs were not met in childhood. An example of failure to address mirroring needs is a parent who talks about her own success in response to her child proudly telling a story about his day and achievements.

Individuals with mirroring-deficient experiences may exhibit behavior that resembles socially oriented perfectionism (see Chapter 1). They may constantly seek affirmation from others to compensate for arrested self-object mirroring needs. They may try to please others at all costs to receive approval. When not receiving affirmation or approval or when perceiving rejection, they may experience intense dread or anxiety and feel fragmented, confused, and abandoned. In essence, they may be hypersensitive to rejection. They may also fear a mirroring shortfall and thus avoid others to prevent rejection.

Individuals with unmet idealizing needs may be prone to idealizing others and may not develop realistic goals. For example, a person with no one real to look up to may be prone to having a grand view of others. By elevating another individual to a perfectionistic state, he or she has created, for the moment, a figure who knows all or can provide protection from harm. He or she may merge with this idealized individual to also feel a sense of superiority. Conversely, the idealizing person may quickly be disappointed when others do not conform to his or her needs or display imperfections. It is thus not uncommon for people to quickly fall from their pedestals.

Another manifestation of stunted idealizing needs is a lack of realistic goals. The individual who does not have a person to idealize does not have a figure whom he or she can incorporate into appropriate goals. The individual may have unrealistic self-expectations and be severely harsh if he or she fails to meet personal expectations, similar to the reaction of a self-oriented perfectionist (see Chapter 1).

TREATMENT AND BEHAVIORAL CHANGE

The central question asked by the therapist influenced by a self-psychological perspective is, "What does the patient need from me now?" The therapist may contemplate whether mirroring, idealizing, or twinship needs are in the forefront when asking this question. When the therapist can understand the patient's needs, he or she has the opportunity to be emotionally attuned to the patient and provide responses that yield further psychological development and emotional regulation. The primary stance of the self-psychological therapist is to decipher the developmental needs of patients and to provide them with appropriate responses.

Similar to the relational therapist, the self-psychological therapist also asks the question, "What is going on between us, the patient and myself, in our therapy relationship?" Although this is a more primary question for the relational therapist, the self-psychological therapist is mindful that he cannot escape his or her subjective experience of the patient. The self-psychologist strives to ensure the patient's self-state is stabilized and self-object needs are addressed and managed before introducing feedback from an outside perspective. Considering that perfectionists are highly sensitive to feedback, this approach can be helpful in maintaining the therapeutic alliance (see Chapter 2). Providing another perspective can also reinforce self-object needs.

Change often takes place, from a self-psychological perspective, by managing therapy ruptures in self-object needs (Kohut, 1984; see also Chapter 2). The therapist inevitably fails to provide perfect attunement or becomes less idealized. At this point, the therapist empathizes with a patient and tries to understand how the misattunement occurred. If the patient and therapist successfully manage the rupture, the patient essentially has a new relationship experience. For example, a patient learns that he or she can be close with the therapist or an authority figure even if he or she is disappointed or feels misattuned. Alternatively, the patient may discover that even if the therapist does not attend to the patient's mirroring needs at times, this does not mean that the therapist does not care about his or her well-being.

In addition, presence, empathy, and understanding of the patient's subjective perspective help repair stunted developmental needs (Kohut, 1971). The affirmation in the therapist's concentrated listening, the patient's experience of affecting the therapist, and the experience of being understood all contribute to providing for developmental needs. The patient gains confidence as feelings are listened to and understood. The therapist, through empathic listening, also enables the patient to integrate disassociated emotions and develop a more differentiated sense of self.

For example, a needy parent may have been unable to tolerate negative emotional states from a child. This parent may have only provided affirmation when the child made pleasing remarks or pursued the parent's thwarted dreams and desires, such as studying to become a lawyer or doctor. Consequently, the patient may have always had to accommodate the parent and may never have had an opportunity for mirroring needs to be met. The patient may not be in touch with genuine feeling about himself or herself. Thus, by mirroring or validating the patient's desires, the therapist can help lead to a more consistent self-concept.

In the remainder of this chapter, case examples are used to exemplify how self-psychology can be effective with perfectionist patients as therapists understand and work with their pathology. The first case example focuses on my work with Andy. Andy has traits consistent with self-oriented perfectionism. She had intense expectations and goals regarding her career aspirations, which when we initially met led her to severe self-punishment and fragmentation.

Andy: The Writer

Andy was a 25-year-old female aspiring to be a film director and screenwriter. She reported that she was seeking therapy because of depression regarding her career goals and anxiety when interacting with others. She taught a class in film theory as an adjunct but overall did not work more than 2 to 3 hours per week. She was entirely supported by her family, about which she expressed feeling guilty and ashamed. The idea of obtaining a part-time job while she was writing was something she considered but eventually dismissed for several reasons. Andy's lack of work experience made her doubt that she could find a job. In addition, she felt she would be too drained to both write and do part-time work. She felt she needed to devote all her time to writing the perfect script. However, at times her high expectations left her with paralysis, and she spent many hours staring at a blank page.

How Andy felt about me or the therapeutic process was often unclear. She was quiet in session, and her affect was constricted. She spoke in a monotone, and I often found it difficult to decipher her needs. Did she need me to be more active or quieter? Should I ask more questions or make more interpretations? Maybe I was making too many interpretations. I shared my confusion with Andy; she smiled and said, "Other people tell me this a lot because I don't

4. Self-Psychology and Perfectionism: Consolidation of One's Sense of Self

provide them with much information. They project their fears and concerns onto me." I replied, "I see, sort of like a therapist." We laughed together, and she explained how she got some measure of pleasure by keeping others off balance. She then discussed how she felt therapists and writers share some traits: Both are observers, and both have an interest in stories and character development. They both try to understand motivation. I validated Andy's observations and perspectives and shared with her my interest in writing. I also shared with her the enjoyment I received in observing others. As our exchange indicates, Andy's primary, or leading edge, needs were those of affiliation, classified by Kohut (1984) under twinship. Andy wanted to identify with me and share our perceived similarities, and my revealing comments conveyed to her the message that we were similar. Feeling connected in this way to someone like me helped Andy shore up and elevate her sense of self, as well as decrease her isolation.

As time went on, Andy's idealizing needs and transference began to emerge more readily. She commented on how brilliant it was that I took on a job as a psychologist. She reported that she was impressed that being in my own business allowed me the time to write and be stimulated by the stories of my patients. I responded to her comments, acknowledging that writing was something I thought of when going into the field. I also joked that when my best seller came out I could get an office overlooking Central Park. We both smiled and laughed after this comment. This intervention was beneficial, because it was a part of a slowly transmuting view of me as someone who was not all powerful yet was not anxious regarding the areas in which I lacked power. Over time, as Andy's idealization of me whittled away, a more realistic view of me developed. She saw me as sturdy with acceptable foibles. This helped her tolerate a more realistic view of herself, as well as of others.

Andy still saw me as strong and safe enough that she could explore her fears and vulnerabilities and discuss her painful past and present with me. She reported that she felt lonely and believed others perceived her as insignificant and unattractive. She was able to trace this back to the lack of affirmation she received in childhood. Andy said she felt she had nothing to offer to people. She wanted to write a great movie so that she would be seen and heard. Her work on the screen would provide her with the affirmation for which she so greatly yearned yet never obtained. A successful movie would make her an admired artist, accepted and respected by others. Her unique vision would be understood. This external validation would support Andy's sense of self. She was hungry for mirroring self-object experiences to fill the void and insecurity that plagued her.

I told Andy that although she desired the affirmation of others, her indifferent presentation and observing stance made it appear that she was not interested in feedback. I repeated what I had previously said regarding my confusion about what she wanted from me. When she pushed people away with a stoic veneer, others could not read or detect her needs. They may also have felt rejected as she stayed in an observational mode. This time, however, Andy did not laugh or joyfully note how she was the mysterious observer in control like a therapist. She looked engaged, concerned, and tearful. Andy reported that she often chose not to express thoughts or feelings because she believed that she would be rejected. She admitted that she did not seek job opportunities because she feared she would be fired. Writing was a place in which she could create her own world. She could control the characters and the responses. I expressed to her that although her withdrawal protected her, it also hid her from others and the possibility of obtaining affirmation, thus perpetuating her isolation and negative self-state feelings. Not only did people possibly disengage, but she missed the opportunity to have her thoughts and feelings heard and continued to feel insignificant. Andy agreed with the consequences of her protective style.

4. Self-Psychology and Perfectionism: Consolidation of One's Sense of Self

Andy was also able to link this style to her relationship with her parents. She stated that while growing up she desired more direct guidance and advice from her parents. She said her mom was depressed and withdrawn. She often spent hours by herself in her room, sleeping or not talking. Andy felt she had nowhere to turn when she had problems. She reported that her mother was religious, and whenever Andy went to her for guidance, she encouraged her daughter to pray or attempted to comfort her by suggesting faith in God. Andy experienced this support as generic remarks that could be applied to anyone; she felt she was misunderstood and was not seen as an important, unique person with productive or positive traits. Andy's mother responded to these needs without expressing that she was hearing, validating, or understanding her daughter's experience.

In addition, Andy reported that she felt her father was emotionally distant. She stated that she was good at photography and singing and wished her father had encouraged her to pursue these tasks. She believed that her father felt offering advice would contaminate her or point her into the wrong direction. Andy experienced this withdrawal as deflating. She did not believe that she was capable of anything significant or had true talents or strengths worth pursuing. She desperately sought external validation and a strong figure to help guide her.

Through our discussion of her interpersonal style and lack of phase-appropriate mirroring, Andy was able to explore other ways of relating in which she stepped out of observation mode and ultimately received more mirroring responses. She felt understood, and I spent a great deal of time in therapy acknowledging her past and pushing her toward future success, such as encouraging her to finish a movie and be proud of her achievement regardless of its material success. As I provided for her developmental needs (twinship, idealizing, and mirroring), she began to flourish and develop realistic goals. Every sentence she wrote did not have to be perfect. She became less judgmental of others as her self-esteem increased. In addition, her maladaptive self-oriented traits significantly decreased.

LISTENING PERSPECTIVES TO FOSTER CHANGE

The case of Andy exemplifies how self-psychology theory can lead to intervention when working with perfectionistic issues that may arise with patients. A specific technique that can further work through obstacles with perfectionist patients is to shift listening perspectives. This technique facilitates change. It developed through self-psychological principles designed to help provide for self-object needs.

The psychoanalyst James Fosshage (1997) introduced the idea of listening perspectives to delineate the modes of listening and thus facilitate growth and the therapeutic alliance. These perspectives are referred to as subject-centered listening and other-centered listening. Subject-centered listening focuses on the patient's perspective and understanding his or her subjective world. An attempt is made to understand the patient's subjective experience and communicate the meaning back to him or her. The patient's feelings, thoughts, and fears are explored and expanded on when the therapist is listening from this perspective. In this mode of listening, a focus on providing self-object needs is often in the forefront. Like the therapist with a self-psychological perspective (described in the earlier section on treatment and behavioral change), the therapist with a subject-centered listening perspective may be asking, "What does the patient need from me?"

In comparison, other-centered listening focuses on how the therapist feels about an interaction. The key question is "How is the patient making me feel?" or, like the second question asked by a self-psychological therapist, "What is happening between us in this therapy relationship?" Is the therapist feeling anxious, seduced, bored, or devalued? Other-centered listening is useful in ascertaining how a patient may contribute to interpersonal dynamics with other people. Both listening perspectives are on a continuum. In other-centered listening modes, the therapist is still often addressing self-object needs. Hearing another's subjectivity can serve mirroring, idealizing, or twinship functions. For example, hearing the opinion of a therapist may provide a patient with a sense of safety. That patient may also become less vulnerable as he or she hears an idea from another subjective perspective that can enrich his or her understanding.

The next case example of Kevin, who displayed other-oriented perfectionism (see Chapter 1), illustrates how shifting listening perspectives can help manage ruptures and facilitate growth. Kevin was seen by a therapist whom I was supervising.

Kevin: A Female Connection

Choosing a Therapist

Kevin was a 37-year-old single male who sought therapy because of depression, feelings of isolation, and loneliness. Although he had friends, he felt disconnected from them and received minimal pleasure from interacting with them. Most of his friends were married with children. He felt that they were from different worlds, and he no longer felt comforted by their compliments and admiration. Kevin spent most of his time running his own business, which initially was rewarding but was now a taxing responsibility with which he was becoming overwhelmed. He desired companionship and a less pressured life.

However, Kevin was chronically disappointed by other people. He felt other people in his life did not meet his expectations. He often felt that they lacked intelligence, were conventional, or were self-centered. Kevin talked about listening to his married friends discuss their pathos, which he felt were trivial and insignificant.

Conversely, he often found it equally unpleasant when his friends talked about their children and success. He believed that their deluded comments were designed to compensate for their insecurities. In essence, he felt quite alone.

When initially consulting my supervisee, a female therapist, via phone, Kevin reported that he was nervous about working with a woman and wanted to know how she worked with male clients. She informed Kevin that she works hard to respect and understand each client's perspective. She acknowledged that her gender may influence ways she thinks about men and the world. This perspective may be helpful at times and less helpful at others. She asked Kevin to give feedback if misunderstanding occurred. Kevin seemed to feel this answer was sufficient and set an appointment. The therapist was curious about why he chose to work with a woman. She filed this question away to ask at a later date.

During the initial phase of treatment, Kevin became frustrated and bothered when his therapist asked about his past or family. Kevin mostly seemed to use the therapy for coaching service for his business. The theme of his business questions revolved around whether he should work with people who proved trustful in the past and the types of boundaries he should set with others.

In her discussions with me, my supervisee was ambivalent about how to proceed and about continuing to provide a problem-solving approach. She contemplated disclosing to Kevin that she felt he was avoiding deeper feelings, and she wondered whether she was too gratifying toward her patient, thus reinforcing his avoidance. We discussed how there may be a parallel process in which the trust that Kevin was asking about in his work situations may apply to Kevin's trust regarding therapy. We thought that waiting and following Kevin's lead before interacting may be beneficial. We agreed that asking him about the therapy relationship and understanding his experience may be the first step.

Overall, Kevin responded to his therapist's interventions and the therapy relationship with great enthusiasm. He raved about his therapist and reported that he greatly appreciated her matter-of-fact approach to his problem. The therapist felt somewhat flattered and perceived what was happening as an idealizing transference. It was conceptualized that Kevin developmentally needed to put her on a pedestal to feel safe.

A Change in Attitude

As the therapist sensed Kevin's growing comfort, she felt she had more room to explore areas about which she was curious. In one session, Kevin proudly informed her about his marketing strategy, which he said objectified women. He seemed proud as he described this to her. His therapist's asked him about his feelings toward women in general. He did not have a response to her question and essentially brushed it off with an "I don't know" remark.

During the next few sessions, Kevin became more withdrawn. He neither sought advice nor was responsive to it, which was typically his and his therapist's mode of interacting. He was also nonresponsive to exploratory questions. He stated that he was dissatisfied with the therapy.

My supervisee thought of providing Kevin with feedback about her experience. She essentially felt as though there was nothing she could do to please him. For a moment, she thought that if she tactfully let him know this, he might gain insight into his interpersonal style and how it affects others. This approach, communicating and listening from an other-centered perspective, would have been consistent with an interpersonal framework (see Chapters 2 and 5). However, she refrained from making this choice. Responding with feedback about her frustration, although possibly accurate and not idiosyncratic, may have caused a deeper rupture with less therapeutic value. She decided to listen from a subject-centered perspective.

Exploring with a subject-centered listening perspective led the therapist to ask Kevin to explain his dissatisfaction in more detail. He reported that he had had so much hope when they first met. He said he felt that he could discuss anything with her; he felt as though his therapist was dynamic and different. However, he explained that he now felt as though she had disappeared and become just like his vision of every other therapist, who nodded and asked textbook questions.

Kevin's therapist validated his feelings of disappointment. She asked Kevin to tell her when he felt that shift had taken place. He reported that it had happened when she asked him to describe his feelings about women. It was his belief that she thought of him as a cliché who hates women because he is not with one. The therapist expressed that his need to feel special in some way was important to him. He became tearful at this. Then Kevin talked about his mother, who he experienced as preoccupied and distracted. He reported that he once tried to break his leg to get her genuine attention. He also described his mother's intense and unpredictable anger as frightening. He felt she was hypercritical and never felt as though he mattered.

The therapist told Kevin that she did not think he hated or disliked women. On the contrary, she said she thought he wanted to connect with women just as he wanted to connect with his mother, that in some way he sought out a female therapist to experiment with achieving this goal. Kevin's affect and capacity to explore and receive his therapist's interpretation suggested he felt understood and may be ready to hear more of her subjective perspective from the other-centered framework. She told him that although she felt he wanted to connect, he was unwittingly pushing her away. He was so concerned that she would disappoint him, like his mother, that any sign of rejection led him to withdraw with anger and thus did not provide him with the opportunity to discuss his hurt feelings. His fear of being disappointed led him to cut people off and devalue them to protect himself. His high expectations of others provided a rationale to avoid intimacy. If people failed him, he moved on and he was safe.

4. Self-Psychology and Perfectionism: Consolidation of One's Sense of Self

Kevin nodded, and it was apparent that a sense of relief had washed over him.

By shifting listening perspectives, the rupture that took place between Kevin and his therapist was restored. In addition, Kevin was able to gain further insight regarding the way he relates with others and how he affects others interpersonally. The interaction between Kevin and this therapist was a new interpersonal experience for the patient, helping him discover how to connect with people rather than push others away.

INTERNALIZING THERAPEUTIC INTERACTION

A key component in helping a patient progress, in addition to what happens during the therapy interaction, relates to the parts of the interaction that are internalized by the patient. The next case example addresses this topic and explores how therapists relate with their patients when they are not in the room with them.

Tracey: The Actress and the Audience

Tracey was a 40-year-old female who came to therapy because she felt stuck in her career. She was a socially oriented perfectionist who avoided career and relationship opportunities fearing she would not live up to expectations. She aspired to be an actress and occasionally obtained roles in commercials and small plays. However, she felt as though she held herself back. She wanted to write a play but could never make the time to do so and could not find the motivation. In her relationships with men, she found herself dating a married man. She appeared perplexed regarding the affair. She reported that at times she was close to him and that at other times her lover pushed her away.

During our initial work together, Tracey and I discussed her tendency in both her career and her personal life to avoid making a commitment. In a sense, she avoided rejection and the risk of not being mirrored or affirmed by the external world. By not throwing herself into writing the screenplay, she did not have to fear facing a disapproving crowd. By not throwing herself into a relationship where long-term intimacy could be established, she did not face rejection by someone truly available. Unfortunately, our discussions about this issue produced little movement.

Another dynamic we discussed was Tracey's need for approval from others. Failing to receive a callback or being dismissed by her boyfriend consistently set off her fears that people wanted nothing to do with her. This led to great self-fragmentation, because the abandonment made Tracey question her sense of self and sent her into great and hopeless despair. Typically, to compensate for this fear of abandonment, Tracey made sacrifices and went out of her way to be pleasing. This behavior included canceling her plans or traveling at late hours to visit her boyfriend.

After being rejected by her boyfriend, Tracey contacted me and requested extra therapy sessions. Initially, I felt ambivalent about providing her with more sessions. On one hand, although not suicidal, Tracey was presenting in a subjective crisis that was affecting her work performance and sleep. On the other hand, I was concerned that gratifying her would induce dependence on me and possibly send a message that she did not have the resources to manage her distress.

Despite my reservations, I decided to grant Tracey more sessions. During these sessions, links between abandonment and lack of mirroring from her family were established. Tracey's parents divorced when she was 5 years old. Tracey waited every other weekend for her father, who did not consistently show up. In the present, she found herself trying to be the perfect and accommodating friend or girlfriend to maintain her relationships. It was helpful for her to make these links, and it appeared that the extra sessions served some positive function. Tracey was able to see her sensitivity toward rejection and her perfectionistic accommodation to prevent rejection.

4. Self-Psychology and Perfectionism: Consolidation of One's Sense of Self

Tracey had a tendency after sessions to email questions about what I had said or to request clarification about items. These questions and her efforts to reach out to me, unlike when she was rejected by her boyfriend, did not seem urgent. I decided to respond to her emails by saying that we could talk about her questions in our next scheduled sessions. In discussing the emails with Tracey, she was able to identify how they were a device to maintain contact with me. What she was searching for was her connection to me, not an answer to the question she was asking. She described how painful it was when I responded to her with postponement. She had fantasies that I would leave or abandon her. She stated that the one thing she liked about acting is an audience applauding her. I validated her feelings and how painful separation was for her. I told her that I could respond to her e-mails by answering but that I felt that true applause for her strength and growth would be for me not to respond. I encouraged her to instead write all her e-mails and questions to me and bring them for the next session. I suggested that sometimes the audience could be with her even when she was alone and that I hoped that she could see that I would be with her as well.

My intervention was designed to satisfy Tracey's developmental need for mirroring, which she was hungry for, as well as to help her internalize our relationship and build independence. By encouraging her to write her emails to me and bring them in the following session, I helped her start to internalize the mirroring function I provided. She was able to experience my validation without my presence, knowing validation would occur in the future. Allowing patients to use self-objects while encouraging internalization of the self-object relationship can be a valuable intervention, and it served Tracey well. In time, Tracey was able to manage her absences from me and others with less anxiety. She was also able to take more risks with her writing and personal life as she explored relationships with partners who were more available.

An Enduring Presence

In therapy, the work does not just happen in the therapy room. Rather, it occurs from the enduring impact of the relationship that exists and is internalized. As mentioned earlier, this internalization was beneficial for Tracey. As another example, a patient who is anxious may internalize the psychological functions of a calm and soothing therapist when under stress. The patient may consciously reflect on the therapist's calm words or demeanor when in a difficult situation outside the therapy room. This is illustrated when a patient says, "I was angry or anxious but thought about what you would say under those circumstances and felt at ease." Thinking about the therapist and incorporating the therapist's ego strength is a valuable aspect of therapy for patients.

In addition, therapists often think of their patients after sessions. Although a therapist may not be incorporating the patient's ego functions, he or she may be moved by content or thoughts that a patient may share in session. With Andy, the patient described in this chapter's first case example, this occurred when I was listening to a Beatles song on the radio. Andy had previously told me that she did not like the Beatles and felt they were overrated and trite. The lyrics that specifically made me think of Andy, "The love you take is equal to the love you make," made me think of how it is hard to see or feel Andy's affection (Lennon & McCartney, 1969). Andy was withholding emotionally and in return was often alone and possibly unloved. I shared my experience of listening to the Beatles song. Andy disagreed that the Beatles equation applied to her. However, she felt moved that I was thinking about her. From a self-psychological perspective, sharing my thoughts served a needed mirroring function. It showed that I thought about Andy and cared about and considered what she said. She existed in my mind and was a part of my world. She was not invisible. It was not so much what I said but rather the process of thinking about her that was important to this patient. Her experience of affecting me was a factor in providing her with cohesion and supporting her sense of self.

Many perfectionists, particularly socially oriented perfectionists, fear they will lose the connection of another person. They try to live up to expectations, real or imagined, because not doing so could leave them abandoned. They fear that if they are not receiving mirroring responses all the time, they will be forgotten and disappear. With these patients, creating an enduring presence experience is thus valuable.

SELF-PSYCHOLOGY IN COMPARISON TO OTHER PSYCHODYNAMIC APPROACHES

The self-psychological model presented here differs from the interpersonal theorist perspective described in Chapter 2, as well as from the Kleinian perspective introduced in the next chapter. A more interpersonal approach may have focused on exploring how the patient impacts the therapist relationally. The therapist may have emphasized how the patient interpersonally connects with others. Alternatively, other models (e.g., Klein) may have explored the client's idealization of her therapist as a defense against aggression and envy.

However, in the example of Andy, focusing primarily on these factors would have prevented me from focusing on what the patient was seeking developmentally, which was her idealizing and twinship needs. By providing for these developmental needs rather than analyzing them as aggression, I allowed Andy to develop a strong alliance to me. In addition, through the slowly transmuting and decreasing elevated view of me and by using humor and our fostered twinship dynamic, she was able to incorporate a healthy, less aggressive stance toward herself and others. Whereas this approach was effective, pointing out defenses to a perfectionist like Andy could have led to resistance and unproductive retaliation.

With Kevin, shifting the listening perspective from other to subject centered was invaluable in restoring the therapy rupture that he experienced with his therapist. Listening just from an interpersonal perspective or other-centered framework, although valuable, may not have repaired the therapeutic conflict that occurred. Keeping in mind Kevin's self-state and self-object needs was necessary before introducing another subjective perspective.

Last, in all psychodynamic approaches, there is a hope that patients internalize the experiences their therapists provide. Object constancy can be reinforced by being explicit that we are thinking about them, which, as mentioned in this chapter, can be beneficial for socially oriented perfectionist patients who fear loss of the therapy relationship.

FIVE

Klein, Perfectionism, and Internal Battles

They say that nobody is perfect. Then they tell you practice makes perfect. I wish they'd make up their minds.

—Wilt Chamberlain

Melanie Klein, a psychoanalyst who worked primarily with toddlers in the early 20th century, is best known for her object relations, or Kleinian, theory. Klein's theory is helpful in understanding perfectionist patients because it addresses the extremes of behavior, which mirror the intensity and extremes that perfectionists experience. This chapter discusses Klein's concepts and how they can be applied when working with perfectionist patients.

KLEINIAN THEORY AND PERFECTIONISM

At the core of Klein's theory is the internal battle people go through regarding love and hate/aggression toward themselves or others stemming from life-and-death instincts. Pathology essentially occurs when a person's aggression and sense of badness and annihilation becomes consuming. This badness overtakes a sense of love and goodness (Greenberg & Mitchell, 1983; Ogden, 1986; Segal, 1964). In addition, aggression and a sense of badness and annihilation can lead to psychic pain. Klein's paranoid–schizoid and depressive positions, concepts of envy and reparation, respectively, can be used to conceptualize, understand, and treat perfectionist patients.

Paranoid–Schizoid Position

Klein believed that the paranoid–schizoid position is the first position into which children are born. At this point, the child has to manage conflict from life-and-death instincts. A sense of destruction and annihilation stems from the death instinct. To manage this self-directed aggression, the child may project this aggression outward and onto the world (Segal, 1964). As a result, the child may experience the world as malevolent and persecutory. The destructive parts of the child are essentially cast out into the world.

In addition, the child may project the life instinct, or goodness, onto another object or source. This idealized source may act as a protector, counterbalancing the aggression from the death instinct and the malevolent world. The child may also hold on to aspects of the life instinct and idealize himself or herself while devaluing objects in the outside world. In the paranoid–schizoid position, the good aspects of oneself or others must be kept separate from the bad aspects at all costs. This separation, called splitting, occurs because good experience objects will be destroyed by bad objects.

Klein also believed that each child is born with a sense of good objects, which are represented by a good breast that feeds him or her, and bad objects, which are represented by a breast that is withholding and does not feed him or her. The child has fantasies about the breasts that provide feedings and about destroying the breasts that do not provide sustenance. When a child receives a good feed from the breast, this reinforces the life instinct and the child's sense of goodness in the world. When the breast is withholding, this reinforces the child's death instinct, and view of world as an evil and dreadful place (Ogden, 1986; Segal, 1964). To an extent, the external reality of good and bad experiences influences the child's development and sense of the world. However, a child's fantasy can magnify or distort experience. A child who has a fantasy about a good feeding breast has intense feelings of goodness if this fantasy then corresponds with a good feed. Conversely, a fantasy about a destructive withholding breast can trump or negate the experience of a good feeding.

When a child has good and responsive parenting, Klein argued, the life instinct is typically reinforced. The child sees himself or herself and others as good and lovable. The child no longer has to rely as much on splitting, because there is enough goodness to offset the badness. However, the child is still prone to move and function in the depressed position, which is described later in this chapter. However, when this does not occur, the good and bad experiences need to be separated.

The extreme of splitting is a dynamic often seen in all types of perfectionist patients. The polarized thinking about self-identity or someone else's identity can explain a perfectionist individual's extreme self-judgment or other-oriented judgment.

Envy

Defenses such as envy occur when a person is functioning in the paranoid–schizoid position. Envy defends against the pain and hopelessness that arises from a person's interaction with good experiences or objects. Envy can occur when a good person or experience is devalued. A person may view someone's goodness or a good experience as unattainable for himself or herself (Greenberg & Mitchell, 1983; Mitchell & Black, 1996; Ogden, 1986; Segal, 1964). The individual may feel dejected, coming to the conclusion that he or she may never possess this goodness. To protect against these negative feelings, the positive attributes of the person or experience are belittled. Thus, not being able to acquire what he or she does not have is no longer a loss (Ogden, 1986; Segal, 1964). For example, no one is typically envious of a neighbor's house if it is viewed as decrepit. People who are prone to envy often have difficulty connecting with something positive or internalizing something as positive. All good is destroyed with envious attacks.

A person may also be envious of herself. In general, she may acquire a goal or an accomplishment. Once she achieves this goal, she may devalue it, or she may be thrown into depression after achieving it. This dynamic may be stimulated because she has anxiety about accepting the good accomplishment. She may fear that it would be difficult or impossible to repeat what she accomplished. She may then devalue the accomplishment, turning it into nothing substantial.

For example, someone who writes a screenplay or achieves success in the music profession may start devaluing these pursuits. She may say to herself or others, "Writing a successful screenplay is just selling out. The whole profession is a waste." This is an example of someone who is displaying envy toward herself, attacking her own goodness. She is left depressed as she continues to strive for the same sense of goodness she spoils.

Envy is a dynamic that can be seen in perfectionist patients. Self-oriented perfectionists may tear down any accomplishments that they make. The envy directed toward their selves makes them continue to feel as though anything they do lacks value. In addition, the extensive and envious devaluing of others can often explain the rigorous standards that perfectionists may have of others. They may devalue and put down others exactly when these people are offering something positive or good.

Depressed Position

In the depressed position, aggressive, hateful impulses are able to coexist with loving impulses. The results of this integration are experiences of guilt and depression (Ogden, 1986; Segal, 1964). For example, a child may experience guilt because the parent whom he aggressively attacked in fantasy is the same parent he realizes he loves. To resolve the ambivalence and guilt, the person often attempts to make reparation, offering a gift or gestures to undo his aggression or harm (Mitchell & Black, 1996; Ogden, 1986; Segal, 1964). To make reparation, the individual must feel as though he can offer enough goodness to outweigh his aggression or badness.

Socially oriented perfectionist individuals often struggle with what appears to be managing the depressed position. The socially oriented perfectionist patient often finds himself or herself giving to and nurturing others. The accommodation can be viewed as reparation to compensate for and overcome a sense of badness. The perfectionist consistently experiences him- or herself in a position in which he or she is compelled to repair a relationship. This can manifest itself as continually doing activities that others like or doing more work in a relationship to manage guilt related to hurting those he or she cares about. Failures to make reparations can lead the individual into deeper despair and possibly a return to the paranoid–schizoid position and splitting. The paranoid-schizoid may describe some socially oriented perfectionists, such as those whose functioning is more paranoid. In these cases, accommodation may stem from avoiding persecution.

TREATMENT AND BEHAVIORAL CHANGE

A patient's capacity to see and tolerate the world as more integrated is a sign of behavioral change from a Kleinian perspective. The patient who is able to rely less on splitting, devaluing, or envious attacks has made progress. Similar to other relational approaches, such as interpersonal psychotherapy and self-psychology (see Chapters 2 and 4), this goal is achieved through the therapy relationship, as illustrated by the case examples that follow. According to Kleinian theory, when the patient is able to internalize good exchanges from the therapy relationship, he or she is able to internalize experiences that reinforce the life instinct. As that person feels and internalizes a stronger sense of goodness, and as that goodness outweighs a sense of badness and the death instinct, his or her need for splitting declines (Mitchell & Black, 1996; Ogden, 1986; Segal, 1964). To a certain extent, the patient learns he or she can repair raptures and is not toxic. When the patient can view himself or herself and others as more integrated, he or she can function more effectively.

Jaden: Guilty Love

Jaden was a 28-year-old male who came for therapy confused about a 4-year relationship in which he was involved. On one hand, he felt secure and content with the woman he was seeing. She was quiet and had a calming influence on him. On the other hand, he found her personality somewhat flat. She had few friends and wanted to spend all her time with him. She became anxious and upset if he did things without her. Jaden felt suffocated by the relationship but could not leave the woman. He feared displeasing her greatly. He often found himself taking an overly accommodating role in his relationship with her and others. His behavior was consistent with a socially oriented perfectionist.

In our therapy relationship, Jaden was also accommodating. When he initially called for therapy, I had few openings and was able to see him only very early, which he expressed was difficult for him. However, he agreed to alter his schedule to see me. I told Jaden that when a later appointment came available I would keep this in mind.

During our sessions, Jaden was never late, never missed a session, and typically agreed with almost everything I said. As the therapy progressed, he asked me again for a later appointment and I realized that for several months I had forgotten to keep this in mind. I apologized and commented that I thought a new appointment time would come up soon. Jaden replied, "No problem at all." However, I thought, "Was it really no problem?" I explored his feelings about my mistake. He again assured me it was a non-issue. He then noted how everyone seems to forget about him.

I commented that I wondered whether his tendency to be overly accommodating induces others, including me, to forget his needs. As usual, he agreed with the interpretation. I gave him feedback that I felt he was afraid to disagree with me or assert his thoughts, fears, or disappointments because it would somehow damage the relationship. Jaden explained that acquiescing was a familiar role for him but that he felt that it was not happening in our therapy relationship.

Several weeks later, I gave Jaden a later appointment. He was quite pleased that I had thought of him and given him the new time. The next week, he bought me an article on a research topic that he was aware I was studying. I thanked him for the gift and accepted it. Although accepting gifts from patients can be often problematic, I thought that it would be appropriate to accept as long as we processed the meaning of his gesture.

When we discussed the article, Jaden talked about how thankful he was and how he felt guilty about changing the time. He felt that he was putting me out in some way by making me change our appointment times. He reported that he was also conflicted about asking me again for a time change. When listening to him, I thought of Klein's depressed position and the concept of reparation. Jaden felt afraid to assert his needs. Doing so made him feel like he was engaging in a hurtful or aggressive act that needed to be repaired. He was ambivalent about what he should do. I expressed that I was happy that he had asked me to change the time because it illustrated assertiveness. His guilt about being assertive and about hurting me by asking for something reminded me of the dynamic he was experiencing in his relationship with his girlfriend, an interpretation I shared. This resonated greatly with him; he reported that he felt his girlfriend would fall apart without him. He could not fathom hurting the person he loved.

Jaden was hypersensitive to doing the wrong things. I asked him about this, and associations to his father came to his mind.

Jaden desperately did not want to be like his father, who was emotionally and physically abusive to his mother. His father ran out on the family when Jaden was 4 years old.

Through our work together, Jaden showed progress toward acting in line with his needs. During one of our sessions, I forgot a personal fact about his life. We were discussing baseball, and I forgot that Jaden had tried out for a minor league team. However, he did not simply brush it off and instead expressed his disappointment. He reported feeling less guilty about expressing his needs. Although he did not want to hurt me, he felt good enough about himself and our therapy relationship that he thought we would both survive.

Overall, Jaden, by always acquiescing, had been attempting to avoid depressive guilt. Understanding his difficulties about guilt over being aggressive (Klein's depressed position) and about asking for what he wants was helpful in exploring and clarifying his dynamics. In the therapy sessions, Jaden began to internalize a greater sense of goodness and to decrease his guilt about being aggressive and assertive. While doing this, he remained empathic and was not looking at things in an extreme and split way. It was helpful to Jaden to create more awareness about his guilt proneness and to have relational experiences in which he was able to experiment with new styles of interaction. Over time, he developed a more integrated and less conflicted sense of self. He consequently was able to break up with his girlfriend and feel less like a toxic and damaging force, one destroying good things and people. His socially oriented perfectionism, to some extent, was ameliorating.

Xandra: Envious Attacks and Splitting

Xandra's First Steps

Xandra was a 30-year-old woman who initially began therapy to manage depression and anxiety. She displayed traits that resembled self- and other-oriented perfectionism. At times, she saw herself as superior and destined for greatness. She had lofty career goals and was quite successful in this area of her life. She never took vacations or missed work, fearing that doing so might hamper her goals. At work, any missed deadline or perceived mistake sent her into a severe tailspin, leaving her depressed for weeks even when there were no objective or tangible negative consequences (self-oriented perfectionism). She also had perfectionistic expectations of others (other-oriented perfectionism) and could be extremely devaluing.

Early in the course of therapy, Xandra displayed insight and was able to make links between her past and her present. She said her career aspirations derived from a desire to compensate for her sense of powerlessness and negative self-view during her childhood. Her family was poor and had barely been able to provide her with the basic necessities. She was ridiculed by peers for wearing ragged clothes that did not fit properly. Financial success and fashion were thus important to her; she wanted to make a flawless impression that conveyed wealth and sophistication.

Xandra described having a difficult childhood. Her father was often fired from jobs because of his drinking. When her father drank, he became physically abusive toward her mother. When this occurred, Xandra found herself cowering in her room, trying to block out the rage. Xandra reported that when she was 8 years old, her father often took her to bars, where he flirted with women and entered into affairs. Her father told her to keep these interactions secret, leaving her confused and depressed. She felt horrible and guilty about hiding his secrets and blamed herself for her parents' difficulties. She reported that her parents divorced when she was 10 and that she saw herself as bad and a burden.

Xandra was highly concerned about whether she would have a successful marriage, and she had difficulty forming intimate relationships. The capacity to form relationships proved to be her primary concern. Our initial work focused on providing her with support, coaching, and nurturing to help her gain the confidence to approach men in the beginning phases of a relationship. She often commented that she wished she could apply the same success and confidence to dating as she did to her career endeavors. She often engaged in promiscuous behavior with men, which she identified as a way to push them away. By sexualizing the relationship, she avoided emotional intimacy.

Through our work together, as Xandra became more aware of her tendencies to sexualize, she began to approach men more adaptively and to have success on dates. She was pleased with this progress and said she was planning on referring everyone she knew to me. However, as her dating relationships progressed, she became devaluing of the men she dated. She ridiculed their lack of knowledge and considered their desire for more contact with her to be needy and desperate. During this phase, Xandra also became devaluing toward me, commenting on the poor décor of my office and her frustration with the therapeutic process. She asserted that she wanted me to just tell her what to do. She expressed that I didn't direct her because I didn't know what to do. These attacks appeared to stem from envy. Just as she was receiving goodness and acceptance from others, she devalued and destroyed them. She was operating in the paranoid–schizoid position.

I validated Xandra's feeling of frustration and explored her feeling of not being provided with the "answers" or "solution" to her problems. She responded with more hostility. I asked whether she noticed the great shift from her desire to refer others to me during one week to her frustration with the therapeutic process the next. She reported that she noticed the shift and was aware that this happened to her occasionally. I commented that it appeared hard for her to hold on to the positive feelings that she had of me and others. She became frustrated with my comments and walked out of the therapy room. She was devaluing me, and I was seen as a bad object.

5. Klein, Perfectionism, and Internal Battles

Two sessions later, Xandra came back, was quiet, and seemed to shrink into the couch. I commented on her reserved behavior. She reported that she had thought about the observation I made about her difficulty in taking in good experiences. A couple of days after our last session, she said had she thought about her childhood, when she had had a problem ingesting food. This occurred when she went out to steak dinners with her father and stepmother. She initially enjoyed these dinners greatly. However, her biological mother often encouraged her not to go and made devaluing comments about her stepmother and father. Her biological mother feared that she would get close to her father and stepmother and that abandonment by her daughter would follow. Xandra reported that she believed throwing up the food was related to the extensive anxiety she had about enjoying the steak dinners. She reported that she could not enjoy the dinner or take in anything good because she feared this was a betrayal of her mother and she would be punished. This developed into a general feeling that she would be persecuted for taking in good experiences. I commented to her that although she is not throwing up food today, she sees in many ways her trouble with ingesting good experiences.

Xandra also revealed that she feared that I would not take her back into therapy after she made disparaging comments. My accepting her back was helpful in letting her experience that her aggression toward me did not destroy me. I informed her that I was here for her and understood that her anger toward me was just half the story. She also expressed feeling guilty about disparaging remarks she made toward men. I asked her about the function of her anger and aggression, and she said that when she is angry, she feels strong and independent. I suggested that to a certain extent her anger makes her feel she does not need anyone. I also stated that when people are of little value, not having them in your life is less of a loss. She agreed with this comment and felt understood. Xandra's guilt about hurting me showed that she was moving her functioning from a paranoid–schizoid position toward a more integrated depressed position.

In time, Xandra was able to see people in a more integrated way as we continued to analyze her tendency to polarize her world. Working through the reparation in our relationship was beneficial. By surviving her aggression toward me, Xandra experienced herself as less toxic. Her ability to repair our relationship built good internalized experiences. If she was able to repair our relationship, then she was not so bad. She may even be able to repair other relationships. My understanding of her also increased our relationship bond, making her feel an increased sense of connection toward herself and me. As time went on, she saw herself as good and, in a more loving way, became less critical of herself and others. Her punishing perfectionism decreased. She found herself relying less on splitting and the defense of envy.

Xandra and the Test

Another aspect of my work with Xandra was passing her therapeutic test. Therapeutic tests are common among patients with perfectionistic tendencies who are prone to judgment. They often put the therapist through a test to assess whether they are going to be negatively judged or misunderstood. In particular, socially oriented perfectionist patients are greatly sensitive to others' opinions and apply such assessment techniques.

During one of our sessions, Xandra asked whether everyone has crazy thoughts. Without much hesitation, I answered, "yes." I told her that occasionally this occurs but that it happens in different degrees for different people. I elaborated, stating that these thoughts can take the quality of aggressive rage, sexual fantasies, and so on. I answered Xandra because she was essentially asking whether I could tolerate her impulses and her fantasies. I wanted to let her know that I was ready. Specifically, she was assessing whether I would devalue or persecute her. After I passed the test, Xandra saw me as safer and was able to reveal more about her anxiety.

Xandra stated that for years she has believed she had a sexually transmitted disease, even though no medical evidence indicates this is the case. She believed that the medical evidence showing she was negative for herpes and HIV was incorrect. She also feared that she may contract another sexual disease from partners. Over time, being informed by Kleinian theory, we looked at this pathology stemming from her sense of badness. She was destructive and spoiled other people if she connected with them because she saw herself as toxic and bad. She alternated from seeing herself as destructive and bad to seeing others as destructive and bad. By passing her test, I had freed Xandra to share these views with me, which in turn helped her become more compassionate toward herself. Thus, any aspect of accepting Xandra helped her accept herself and ameliorate her aggression toward herself and her sense of badness.

Perfecting the Process

My treatment of Xandra was helped a great deal by using the Kleinian framework. However, looking back, we can question the timing of my comments and interpretations. At times, it can be effective to tailor interpretations and comments so that they are consistent with the patient's apparent functioning in the depressed position or the paranoid–schizoid position. For example, I made an interpretation to Xandra that she may be incapable of holding on to positive experiences and was displaying contradictory behaviors toward me (idealizing me one week and devaluing me the next). Although possibly accurate, my interpretation was done while Xandra was functioning in the paranoid–schizoid position. Consequently, any comment or interpretation she received was prone to be viewed in a polarized fashion. Thus, confronting her with something confrontational could exacerbate her paranoid anxiety. This appeared to occur; she saw my comment as devaluing, which caused her to retreat and to withdraw from therapy for 2 weeks. This comment could have been more helpful and easier to digest if she had been functioning in the depressed position, had a higher capacity for integration, and been less prone to splitting.

However, we can conclude that for some patients, accurate interpretations about their functioning can be stabilizing, leading them to a more integrated way of functioning. Maybe Xandra needed to be pushed to devalue me before she could integrate her feelings toward me. It may be difficult to gauge what will work with each patient at each moment. A helpful technique therapists could employ is to ask about patients' interpretation of the therapists' feedback and subsequent feelings about the feedback regarding their defenses or functioning. This can be beneficial when working with perfectionist patients. It allows therapists to gauge and intervene appropriately in the patients' interpretations of their comments. If I had asked Xandra how she felt about me commenting on her capacity to hold on to positive experiences, she may have given me feedback that I could have worked with in that moment, granting me the opportunity to neutralize aggression she may have been experiencing.

INTEGRATION OF PSYCHODYNAMIC APPROACHES WITH PERFECTIONISTS

We have now looked at treating perfectionist patients from three perspectives: interpersonal (see Chapter 2), self-psychological (see Chapter 4), and Kleinian (described in this chapter). All of these schools of thought place great value on the therapy relationship and the patient growing from the dynamics that occur within it. All three approaches also emphasize something that the patient does not engage in typically with other people but that occurs in the therapy relationship. This new experience with the therapist then generalizes to the patient's outside world.

Although some parallels can be drawn from the various schools of thought, there are some differences in how each school conceptualizes perfectionist patients. The interpersonal school looks at relationships and at balancing secure interpersonal styles that reduce anxiety against satisfying interpersonal styles that exacerbate anxiety. The self-psychological perspective conceptualizes patients as striving to achieve a stable sense of self and meet developmental needs. Finally, the Kleinian school views patients as having to manage conflict between good and bad objects. The type of approach the therapist embraces affects the conceptualization and language that he or she uses with the patient.

How can these differences be integrated? One approach that can be utilized across all psychodynamic approaches when working with perfectionist patients is to be cognizant of listening perspectives (see Chapter 4). For example, when listening to a patient, the therapist can consider that patient's level of cohesion. Does he or she need validation because of feelings of insecurity, or is he or she stable and able to hear the therapist from an other-oriented perspective? In Kleinian language, this approach can be seen as considering whether the patient is more cohesive and integrated (in the depressed position) or less integrated (in the paranoid–schizoid position). Conceptually, giving a perfectionist patient feedback when he or she is more integrated or is feeling a higher level of esteem may be more effective considering his or her sensitivity. In addition, asking about reactions to feedback and how the patient is experiencing interpretations can be extremely helpful, because it is often unclear how patients are precisely processing information.

Another valuable approach when working with perfectionist patients, regardless of the theoretical framework, involves therapists taking responsibility for how they may be contributing to the dynamic. When working with perfectionist patients, being able to acknowledge imperfections constitutes productive modeling. Seeing therapists acknowledge imperfections can convey that the patients can also accept their imperfections.

Choosing one approach over another can affect what is and what is not explored. Which approach is best? To answer this question, therapists can view listening to a patient like listening to music. Does the patient's story have the tragic quality of battling good and evil? Does aggression seem to permeate the patient's life? Does the patient seem to attack all goodness? These overtones may sound like notes that suggest a Kleinian framework. Conversely, the patient's story may consist of themes of yearning to be seen and heard. Or the patient may be desperately looking for a mentor or guide to protect and identify with. Both impressions suggest that a self-psychological framework may apply. Finally, the patient's story may have themes of interpersonal restriction and fear of losing a relationship connection that may illicit a more relational understanding. The patient may also have a combination of stories, which over time evolve with multiple layers that require multiple ways of listening and frameworks. Keeping this in mind and listening attentively to music of a patient's story can help in connecting effectively with him or her and engendering change.

SIX

Mindfulness and Buddhist-Influenced Techniques

*I think perfectionism is based on the obsessive
belief that if you run carefully enough, hitting each
stepping-stone just right, you won't have to die.*

—Anne Lamott, Bird by Bird: Some Instructions on Writing and Life

This chapter explains how Buddhist principles and mindfulness can be applied to help facilitate work with perfectionist patients. It includes a brief discussion of the noble truths. It also explains how mindfulness techniques help patients who crave perfectionistic states and ideals let go of rigid frameworks. Ways in which mindfulness and Buddhist-informed concepts can be superimposed or integrated into psychodynamic approaches when working with perfectionist patients are also addressed.

NOBLE TRUTHS

Noble truths are the four basic doctrines that form the backbone of Buddhism (Epstein, 1996). They are believed to be at the center of the Buddha Gautama's first postenlightenment teaching. The first two speak to the pathology of perfectionism, and the final pair gives insight into potential ways to treat perfectionist patients.

Dukkha and Its Cause

The first noble truth is referred to as *dukkha*. It asserts that life is dissatisfaction. According to dukkha, we are all subject to decay and humiliation. Nothing is permanent, and all things will fall short of our standards. As we age, our health will decline, loved ones will pass, and beauty will fade. We may also fail to love or be loved. No matter how hard we strive to obtain satisfaction, all that we hold dear will dissipate (Epstein, 1996).

The second noble truth refers to craving and how it can cause suffering. One aspect is a craving for certainty. The craving can manifest itself in convictions, for example, that there is a heaven or that there is no afterlife. The philosophers during Buddha's time described this dichotomy as externalists, who believed in a heaven or a real self, versus annihilationists, who believed in the futility of life and meaningless (Epstein, 1996).

These truths raise two important questions: What does the perfectionist crave, and how does denial of the decay that is elemental to dukkha affect perfectionists' functioning and pathology? The socially oriented perfectionist patient desperately craves the approval of others. If such a person contorts and bends to the wishes of others, he or she will continue to be seen as worthy and valuable. He or she holds on to the fixed idea of a caretaker or a giver. The person continues to exist as he or she continues to please. In contrast, the self-oriented perfectionist remains rigidly focused on accomplishing great goals. If milestones are accomplished and achieved, the person is affirmed. This person's craving is to never fall short of his or her ideals. For the self-oriented perfectionist, falling short is unacceptable, is humiliating, and means utter failure. Finally, an other-oriented perfectionist craves the perfect image of another. If others do not meet his or her ideal image or expectation, they are devalued and disregarded.

From a Buddhist perspective, the quest for perfection is lack of awareness that nothing remains and that decay is inevitable. The craving for a fixed ideal image leads to suffering and pathology.

The ideal states are fantasies and illusions and are an attempt to grasp security or certainty.

Epstein (1996) describes the myth of Narcissus, which exemplifies the plight of the perfectionist. Narcissus, a young Greek, finds his reflection in the water and is awestruck by the beauty he sees. He is unable to leave the reflection and desires to hold on to this fixed ideal of beauty and perfection. The image cannot be held on to and decays, as we all do. Narcissus does not eat or move from the reflection, and he eventually wilts and decays with the image. The craving to remain with the ideal prevents Narcissus from experiencing the love of others willing to embrace him.

TREATMENT AND MINDFULNESS MEDITATION

Thinking Categorically

When people think about their experiences, they tend to put things into categories such as good or bad. When they do something wrong, they may describe themselves as stupid and unworthy. When blocked from a goal, they may describe the people or obstacles faced as mean or unfair. When they become worried, sad, or rejected, they may refer to themselves as anxious, depressed, or unattractive. Overall, these categorical thoughts or judgments can trap people into negative mood states and prevent them from seeing that their thinking is biased and unclear.

When people describe feeling, states, or thoughts about themselves as facts, they are not being mindful. Someone can feel sad after being rejected, but that does not mean he or she is a depressed person who will never meet anyone. To be mindful is to be aware that feelings and thoughts are experiences that come and go. Being mindful consists of being aware that a feeling of being a failure does not make someone a failure. When a person becomes fused with internal feelings or thoughts, these feelings become amplified, leading to more distress. By recognizing thoughts and feelings in a nonjudgmental way as passing experiences, one can release them. The person rejected may feel hurt and depressed but can still recognize these as feelings that will pass. For example, such a person may see that she is not her feelings but rather is an entity just experiencing them. She becomes more decentered from thoughts and feelings.

Kabat-Zinn's (1994) mountain visualization helps people comprehend mindfulness: A mountain experiences rain, snow, or sleet that covers its terrain. The mountain, however, is a large conglomeration of rocks and soil, not the weather states it experiences.

Accepting and Embracing Feelings

The perfectionist who does not achieve a goal often judges this as a failure and berates himself or herself. This type of person feels defeated when not achieving a goal and becomes that feeling of defeat. To manage negative mood states, a perfectionist often engages in more striving behavior to achieve personal goals and compensate for negative feelings without acknowledging them. In contrast, mindfulness allows such an individual to experience feeling and thoughts without pushing them away (Linehan, 1993; Williams, Teasdale, Segal, & Kabbat-Zinn, 2007). Permitting oneself to experience thoughts and not cut them off leads to integration.

Denying emotions such as sadness and anger contributes to their continuation (Linehan, 1993). They come back stronger or leak out in other areas of the person's life. Substance use, repetition of negative patterns, and avoidance are all strategies people may use to manage and suppress or deny emotions. In the long run, this is not adaptive (see the section on perfectionism and adaption in Chapter 1). Not acknowledging anger, for example, can manifest into depression, and depression can lead back to anger. We can view mindfulness as an exposure treatment similar to a behavioral treatment for a phobia, in which the person acknowledges and then faces the fear. The person who is depressed or anxious, for example, acknowledges his depression or anxiety, exposes himself to the pain, and refrains from blocking the experience. He survives the feeling just as someone afraid of elevators survives traveling to a high floor. After surviving and facing the emotion, it dissipates. He learns that he is not his emotion.

Staying in the Moment

When working with patients with perfectionism, I actively explain the concept of mindfulness, because being judgmental and thinking categorically are fundamental aspects of their struggle. I may review some Buddhist principles with them to explain the etiology of mindfulness. I then teach and have them engage in mindfulness breathing exercises.

When practicing mindful breathing, patients focus on their breath and the physical sensations of their stomach rising and falling. They then label thoughts, feelings, or distractions that come to mind. As their therapist, I attempt to be nonjudgmental when I notice their minds are distracted. I tell them to not push out distracting thoughts but rather, after noticing, gently bring their attention back to their breath. The idea is for patients to be mindful of their breath, focusing on this one activity and becoming aware when they are distracted. A key component of mindfulness is attempting to focus on one thing in the moment (Williams et al., 2007).

Perfectionist patients generally find the mindful breathing exercise relaxing. More important, they learn how to apply mindfulness not only to their breath but to the rest of their life as well, whether they are walking, talking, or reflecting on their thoughts. If the perfectionist can learn to apply mindfulness to his or her rigid thoughts, he or she can see them as just thoughts, not rigid rules that must be lived up to all the time. The person can see that thoughts and ideals are transient concepts that decay in time. This self-view is illustrated in the case example of Craig.

Craig: The Craver

Filling Mother's Shoes

Craig was a young, good-looking 27-year-old male who came to see me for therapy because he felt dissatisfied in his relationships with women. He was unable to find a woman who lived up to his standards. After having sex with a woman, he moved on to the next female. In every woman he dated, Craig found some type of flaw. He rarely saw the women he met as attractive or intellectually stimulating. He reported that in the past he would have sex with women and then entertain his friends with the tales of his debauchery. As time passed, however, his friends started marrying or getting engaged. Craig started to become anxious about whether he would ever find someone and decided to enter therapy.

Craig described having a good childhood despite his mother passing away when he was 9 years old. He reported that his father was always there for him emotionally and financially. He had fond memories of his mother, whom he described as beautiful. He recalled going to the bank one day with his mother at the age of 7. A man stared and commented on her appearance. The man said to him, "You have an attractive mom." He recalled that his mom, upon hearing this comment, grabbed his hand tightly. This memory was significant to him for reasons he had difficulty articulating. He also reported having some learning issues and difficulty reading when growing up and expressed that his mother was extremely encouraging, supportive, and nurturing. He talked about missing his mother greatly. His affect was constricted and distant when talking about her. He often commented that the women he met could not live up to his mother's expectations.

During the initial sessions, Craig said he mostly had superficial and purely physical relationships with women. He felt somehow that having sex with so many different women was making him feel empty and more alone. He expressed concerns that this experience may be contributing to a tendency to devalue and objectify women. He decided that he no longer wanted to have one-night stands. He was also motivated to decrease his drinking and marijuana smoking. He asked me what I thought about this plan, and I agreed that it sounded sensible.

While listening to Craig's issues, I thought about the noble truths and how he was craving an ideal, something certain that would satisfy him. I thought he was looking for the perfect mother-type figure and haunted by his loss, trying to undo it. Could I help him mourn his loss? Could I help him live with dissatisfaction and help free him, like Narcissus, from staring into a body of water for the perfect illusionary image? His other-oriented perfectionism and ideals that no one could live up to were keeping him trapped. Was he devaluing women with the fear that engaging in another relationship was a betrayal to his mom? I kept these questions in the back of my mind as I tried to stay emotionally present to Craig.

During one of our sessions, Craig asked me for concrete advice. He reported that he did not want psychobabble, just my opinion. He stated that he had a date coming up. He was set up by a friend and was somewhat optimistic about the date. However, he was concerned because he was not sure how it was going to go and did not want to upset the friend who arranged the date if it went go badly. I responded, looking at his request as a cue for an impromptu lesson on mindfulness.

I told Craig that he should try to go into the date without expectations about the future. I told him to be present and to focus on connecting. I suggested that he become aware if he felt distracted or found he was being judgmental. His task, I said, was to get to know his date and to have her learn about him. Preconceived notions or judgments about her intelligence or beauty could interfere with him attending to the experience. I told him to notice whether he felt judgmental or distracted and to bring his attention back to the task of learning about each other. Craig seemed pleased with this suggestion. He said my advice took away the pressure of trying to be something that he was not ready to be.

In the therapy session after his date, Craig expressed that he had a good time and felt connected. He said trying to stay in the moment was helpful. However, a session later, he reported that he had gone on another date with the woman and did not have a good time. We discussed why this occurred. The night before the date, he went out drinking and then slept the whole day until the date occurred. He acknowledged that being hungover and irritable from drinking may have greatly affected his ability to enjoy the date. Nonetheless, his interest in the woman had decreased significantly, and he was debating whether he would see her again.

I found it interesting that Craig went out drinking the night before his date, and I asked whether he felt that on some level he did not want the date to go well and had been sabotaging it. Did part of him want it to fail? Were the fears associated with intimacy such as loss? While Craig could logically resonate with the questions, he denied that he felt such possibilities could be relevant. It felt as though we were at a stalemate. Craig was able to see how he may be pushing women away through his sexualized behavior and drinking, but he was missing a real emotional connection to part of himself. I believed that his issue was connecting to his emotions. I believed that a good start to this would be to get him to connect with his breath.

Embracing Anger

For many months, Craig and I did mindful breathing exercises at the beginning of our therapy sessions. Craig was able to focus on his breath and label thoughts and feelings that came up during the process. He was learning to separate thoughts from facts and to not fuse himself with his thoughts. If a feeling came up, he was able to acknowledge it as a feeling and refocus on his breath. After some time, I proposed a slightly different mindfulness exercise. I requested that he focus on whether, when something came to mind, his thoughts were sad or happy. I instructed him to create the mental space to experience whatever came to mind without pushing it out. I instructed him to accept all of his thoughts compassionately.

Craig practiced this exercise for a couple of weeks. One day, while focusing on his breathing during a therapy session, he started to cry. He verbalized his sadness during the exercise, and I instructed him not to push it away but rather to let it in and to remain receptive and open to his sadness. After the exercise, we discussed what had happened. He reported that he had thought about his mother and how much he missed her. He also mentioned feeling angry during the exercise and ashamed to voice his anger toward his mother. Craig was angry that by dying she had left him. He was angry that he could no longer hold on to her and be protected by her loving embrace. As he experienced his sadness and anger, I encouraged him to continue to embrace and mindfully attend to these feelings.

As time passed, Craig was able to see that his perfectionistic attitude toward women was stemming from his displaced anger toward his mother, who had tragically left him. However, more important than his intellectual insight were his connection to and his emotional integration of his anger. He was no longer denying or suppressing his anger. Embracing his anger emotionally and observing and watching it with all his senses helped him let go of it and experience it in a less fused way. As he began to accept his anger, his severe ideals and expectations regarding women declined. He became more compassionate. As he mourned and let go of the hurt and anger toward his mother, Craig was able to approach others from a more giving place, where he was open to both love and risk.

Like Craig, many perfectionist patients feel vulnerable or judgmental about having certain emotions. Consequently, they may not allow themselves to feel their emotions. They often are resistant to any type of mindfulness exercise, which promotes accepting and experiencing thoughts and feelings, as well as letting go of them. Their resistance to doing the exercise ironically indicates why it may be valuable for them to engage in mindfulness. As illustrated here, by using mindfulness, Craig was able to gain more insight into the dynamics of his anger toward women. The mindfulness approach helped soften his defenses and anxiety when it came to expressing and acknowledging emotions.

MINDFULNESS AND COUNTERTRANSFERENCE

Using mindfulness skills also greatly affects how the therapist listens to the patient.

When a therapist is not mindful but rather preoccupied or putting the patient's comments into categories such as right or wrong, the therapist may be cut off from hearing the richness of the patient's subjective perspective. For example, if I, as the therapist, am angry about an interaction outside of the therapy, not letting go of that anger affects how I attend to a patient's emotional states. In addition, if a patient is sharing on a topic that I disapprove of or to which I have a personal reaction, this impedes my capacity to maintain a subject-centered listening stance (see Chapter 4).

As an example, consider a self- and socially oriented perfectionist patient I refer to here as Nate. During one of our therapy sessions, Nate described an aspect of his progress that he deemed helpful for himself. He had been reading philosophy, taking aspects of what he learned regarding mindfulness, and considering the idea of doing away with good and bad. He reported that these human-made categories were subjective and influenced by who is in power. As he talked about this process, I noticed myself becoming distressed and concerned. If Nate was doing away with good and bad, did this give him the license to act like a sociopath? I had the urge to engage in a conversation about ethics, morals, and Kant's moral imperative to anchor him. I became mindful of this urge and these thoughts, and I labeled my feeling, thoughts, and judgments as anxiety. I listened as Nate explained spontaneously that by not having categories of good and bad, he was able to view himself more compassionately. He also felt more compassion toward others as he felt less shame and guilt about his identity. He reported that he had been trying to explain this concept to me for a long time and finally felt like I understood. Letting my anxiety pass and refraining from giving a philosophical lecture on right and wrong was thus helpful.

At times, therapists may experience perfectionist patients as rigid, aggressive, or disrespectful. Managing these feelings in a mindful way, rather than acting on them impulsively, can be helpful. In addition, mindfulness in how therapists' operate therapeutically can be a model for patients to incorporate as a part of their psychological well-being. The therapists' presence can be a guide that patients such as Jason, the focus of the next case example, can emulate.

Jason: Mindfulness and Compassion

Jason was a 30-year-old man who was intensely self-critical. He had a brittle self-view, and to compensate for weaknesses, he strove to do things perfectly regarding almost all areas of his life. He exercised incessantly and ate extremely carefully because he abhorred being overweight. In reality, however, he was significantly underweight and in quite good shape. Jason's feelings of being unattractive often negatively affected his sexual activity with his girlfriend. He avoided having sex with her, fearing that he would not be able to please her sufficiently. When having sex, he became insecure about his physical appearance. In general, being naked was difficult for him.

In social settings, Jason always had anxiety about going to a new store or restaurant, fearing that there would be some protocol he would fail to follow. He never wanted to ask for help from others. At work, he never asked for assistance on projects. He felt as though he should know all the answers or be able to figure them out on his own. He would rather spend hours researching a topic than simply ask a coworker who may have the answer. He excelled at work and received many promotions. However, he was never satisfied; he always had a sense that he should accomplish more and was not moving up fast enough.

Jason had insight that his self-directed anger and critical stance toward himself stemmed from his childhood. Jason's father, an ex-marine, separated from his mother and the house when Jason was 12 years old. He made little contact with Jason after leaving the home. Jason consequently felt abandoned and unloved. He reported that when he lived with the family, his father had been verbally abusive. He stated that if he was a minute late for dinner or an activity, he was yelled at and scolded intensely. Jason believed that there was no pleasing his father. He also felt extremely jealous, because he believed that his father favored his half-brothers and half-sisters.

In our work together, Jason began to acknowledge that his anger toward his father was self-directed and internalized. His perfectionism was a self-punishment, as well as a hope to finally reach a good-enough state of being. Jason thought that if he could accomplish a certain level of greatness, he could have peace of mind.

Jason, like many self-oriented perfectionists, had a harsh and punitive stance toward himself. Mindfulness and meditation can be helpful in reducing this self-punishment. Therefore, I used mindfulness techniques throughout my work with Jason. I felt specifically that a compassion mindfulness meditation would be beneficial. I used the following meditation in one of our therapy sessions in the hope that Jason could further learn to let go of his aggression toward himself. This meditation is from Kornfield (2008).

Compassion Meditation

- Sit breathing softly.
- Feel your body.
- Treasure your life.
- Notice the way you guard yourself.
- When you are ready, bring to mind someone you love.
- Picture them and feel your natural caring for them.
- Be aware of their measure of suffering.
- Recite: "May you be held in compassion, may your pain be eased, and may you be at peace."
- Turn the compassion toward yourself.
- Recite: "May I be held in compassion, may my pain be eased, and may I be at peace."

After several weeks, Jason came to one of our therapy sessions and talked about having a moving experience after doing the compassion exercise. He reported that, for some reason, he thought of his father while doing the exercise. He was somewhat perplexed that this image came to mind because of his intense displeasure with his dad. However, he did not suppress the imagery of his father and mindfully accepted and followed his train of thought. He described memories of his father and recalled images in which his father taught him everything about cars and how to fix them. On weekends, they spent hours getting parts for his father's car collection and rebuilding engines. He stated that his father's skill and patience with him helped him become mechanically inclined and contributed a great deal to his ability to fix anything, which he greatly valued. Jason also reported that his father's work ethic and determination were traits he has emulated, ones that led to his great success at work and promotions. Jason reported that he felt sad for his father, who was physically abused by his grandfather, and felt that his dad had tried to do the best he could. He reported feeling guilty about not opening or responding to letters that his dad sent after his parents' divorce.

Jason reported that he felt his father was not a monster like his mother made him out to be. He was able to acknowledge his father's flaws but in subsequent sessions developed a more integrated view of his father, which was greatly triggered by the compassion meditation. As our therapy progressed, Jason was also able to develop a more integrated and compassionate view toward himself. He became more tolerable regarding what he deemed as falling short of his expectations and accepted his foibles while acknowledging his strengths. He still wanted to be perfect but did not punish himself for falling short of his ideals.

SEVEN

Cognitive Therapy and Perfectionism

*Out of the crooked timber of humanity, no straight
thing was ever made.*

—Immanuel Kant

Cognitive-behavioral therapy posits that thoughts and beliefs about the world affect a person's mood and functioning (Beck, 1995). In this chapter, cognitive therapy approaches are described, along with techniques targeting patients with perfectionist traits.

PATHOLOGY OF PERFECTIONISM

Belief Layers

In cognitive therapy, there are three layers of beliefs and thoughts that are related to and influence one another: core beliefs, intermediate beliefs, and automatic thoughts.

Core beliefs are often nonconscious, fundamental views a person has about the world and self (Beck, 1995). These beliefs are shaped by significant others (caretakers, peers, and parents) and life experiences. A person with nurturing parents and positive affirmation will likely develop the core beliefs that he or she is good and that others view him or her positively. These beliefs contribute to security and safety. Conversely, a person exposed to neglecting and rejecting parents may develop core beliefs that he or she is bad and incompetent. This person may view others as untrustworthy.

Intermediate beliefs are rules, assumptions, and attitudes a person has about personal core beliefs (Beck, 1995). For example, the patient with the core belief that he is bad may have an intermediate belief, or rule, that he must do everything perfectly to be accepted. This intermediate belief could lead to compensatory behavior, such as striving to please others all the time, as often seen with socially oriented perfectionists.

Automatic thoughts are beliefs about a particular situation that is influenced by core and intermediate beliefs (Beck, 1995). For example, a young man may have been denied when asking a girl to go out on a date with him, despite all of his attempts to win her over with his humor. This man's automatic thought is that rejection from one woman means he must be unattractive to all women. This belief affects the man's mood significantly, and he becomes depressed.

Cognitive Conceptualization

As illustrated, distorted automatic thoughts and core beliefs can lead to pathology in people prone to perfectionism. Perfectionists typically have rigid, all-or-nothing thinking. Perfectionist individuals also tend to have common beliefs that center on acceptance, standards, and the importance of being perfect. Cognitions such as "Others won't like me unless I excel," "People expect nothing less than perfection for me," and "Everything I do must be perfect" are common. One way to begin to understand and treat cognitions is to create a cognitive conceptualization for the patient.

Reconsider the earlier example of the young man denied a date. He had a core belief that he is unlovable. Intermediate beliefs, such as "I have to be funny all the time," led to the compensatory behavior, or strategy, of always trying to make jokes to win others' affection. Ironically, others—including the girl who refused to go out with him—experienced the man's tendency to be humorous all the time as overbearing, which ultimately contributed to his isolation. This isolation and a single date rejection led him to form the automatic thought that he is unattractive to all women.

Thus, we can see this young man's progression from a core belief to an intermediate belief, a compensatory strategy, and finally the situation that in turn led to his automatic thought and subsequent pathology. This progression can be easily visualized through the use of a cognitive conceptualization diagram, as demonstrated by looking again at the previous chapter's case example of Jason.

Jason: Revisited

Recall Jason, the self-critical 30-year-old male I initially described in Chapter 6. In brief, his cognitive conceptualization was as follows. Jason had experienced verbal abuse in his childhood and felt abandoned after his father left when Jason was 12. Jason developed core beliefs that he was inadequate and ugly. His intermediate belief was that if he was not perfect, he had fallen short. To compensate, he felt he had to have a perfect body, avoid displaying a lack of knowledge in any specific area, and always be perfect in his work. These compensatory strategies led, as mentioned in Chapter 6, to sexual difficulties, sexual performance anxiety, and depression related to self-punishment. Table 7.1 maps the cognitive conceptualization just described.

The rest of this chapter uses Jason and his cognitive conceptualization to illustrate many of therapy techniques that can be used when working with perfectionist patients. As mentioned in Chapter 6, mindfulness was instrumental in helping Jason achieve balanced thinking. I was also guided greatly by cognitive conceptualization, as shown in Table 7.1, and cognitive therapy, as explained in the next section. Overall, I used an integrated approach when working with Jason.

TABLE 7.1
Cognitive Conceptualization Diagram

Relevant childhood data
Jason experienced verbal abuse by his father
His father was not always present.

⇓

Core beliefs
Jason believes he was not good enough
He is inadequate
Others will perceive him as inadequate
He was ugly

⇓

Intermediate beliefs
I must be perfect in everything that I do

⇓

Compensatory strategies
Extensive physical exercise
Never asking people for assistance
Checking over work excessively to prevent mistakes
Consistently be entertaining and interesting
Having sex in dark places to minimize his body from others

⇓

TREATMENT OF PERFECTIONISM

Treatment of perfectionism from a cognitive therapy perspective consists of changing rigid, all-or-nothing thoughts to more balanced and realistic ones. By changing someone's thoughts, the therapist can change the person's behavior and negative mood states. Motivating patients to change their way of adapting to their environment is also a crucial aspect of the treatment. Many techniques, including dialectical thinking, cognitive restructuring, and pie charts, can be implanted when working with perfectionist patients to change their thought and adaptation patterns. In addition, behavioral techniques and experiments can be integrated with psychodynamic techniques.

Dialectical Thinking

While developing a cognitive conceptualization of Jason (see Table 7.1), I gave him simultaneous feedback based on the conceptualization. We also discussed his perfectionism collaboratively. Research illustrates that giving feedback to perfectionist patients in a matter-of-fact and objective, dispassionate style can significantly decrease perfectionism in individuals. This style is similar to motivational interviewing and dialectical approaches.

In a dialectical framework, both positive and negative aspects of patients' dynamic and behavior are recognized. In therapy, the dialectical framework consists of validating that it makes sense for patients to adapt as they do but that they could change how they do things (Linehan, 1993). "I love you, you're perfect, now change" is the underlying principle of the dialectical stance regarding therapy.

In talking about Jason's perfectionism, I followed many of the concepts and used much of the language common in the dialectical framework. For example, to a large extent, Jason did not want to give up his excessive standards or his overchecking and avoidance strategies. I validated and accepted the function of his compensatory strategies. He was extremely engaged as we discussed the function, in detail, of strategies such as working out. "Working out makes me feel good and in control," he stated. He would smile when addressing the positive function of his compensatory style and said to me at one point, "I guess I don't need therapy." I replied, "The hell with therapy," and we both laughed.

Allowing Jason the space to acknowledge the satisfaction he received from and the security in his compensatory strategy helped him address the other role and desire for change. My irreverent response led him to talk about the negative consequences of his compensatory strategies. These included injuries and the amount of time he spent engaging in exercise, which took away from other activities. This intervention was helpful in increasing motivation, managing resistance, and having him accept and embrace tools for dealing with his acute symptoms.

As the pros and cons of Jason's compensatory strategies were assessed and his motivation for change increased, we moved into the more active skill of cognitive restructuring. Modifying automatic thoughts is often the first step in cognitive restructuring.

Cognitive Restructuring

Conducting cognitive restructuring requires first having the patient identify situations that create negative automatic thoughts and thus negative mood states (Beck, 1995). For Jason, negative mood states were related to concerns about mistakes or falling short of ideals. When he felt as though he had made a mistake, he became anxious or depressed. However, the automatic thoughts he had about situations regarding his performance were often irrational. Going back to the cognitive conceptualization of Jason, as seen in Table 7.2, show that his automatic thought about career failure stemmed from core beliefs related to inadequacy.

Helping Jason identify irrational automatic thoughts and develop more rational responses led to more balanced thinking and more positive mood states. Table 7.3 shows a thought log that restructures Jason's irrational automatic thought. The log illustrates a situation that elicited emotions caused by his automatic thought. The log also illustrates the rational response that Jason is led to through questioning. He addressed these irrational thoughts in therapy and through homework.

Like automatic thoughts, core beliefs and intermediate beliefs can be restructured, because they are the roots from which automatic thoughts stem. Restructuring the roots, however, often takes time, because these roots develop from years of behavioral experience. Sometimes exploratory therapy and more dynamic approaches are necessary to make changes in core beliefs.

TABLE 7.2
Cognitive Conceptualization Diagram

Relevant childhood data
Jason experienced verbal abuse by his father
His father was not always present

⇓

Core beliefs
Jason believes he was not good enough
He is inadequate
Others will perceive him as inadequate
He was ugly

⇓

Intermediate beliefs
I must be perfect in everything that I do

⇓

Situation
Making a mistake on a memo

⇓

Automatic thoughts
I will not succeed in my career

TABLE 7.3
Cognitive Restructuring Log

SITUATION	EMOTIONS	AUTOMATIC THOUGHT (COGNITIVE DISTORTION)	RATIONAL RESPONSE	OUTCOME
I made a mistake in a memo I wrote at work	Sadness and anxiety	I am not intelligent and will not succeed in my career	Making a mistake does not mean I am a failure	Decreased anxiety and sadness as rational response is identified

Secondary Processing

When working with perfectionist patients on cognitive restructuring, it is important to address secondary processing. This occurs after a patient has and then replays an irrational automatic thought.

For example, during one session, Jason expressed that he believed he had made a mistake when giving a presentation at work and that the presentation he gave had been boring. This thought was triggered by seeing someone yawn while he was talking, leading to anxiety. He had been replaying this scene repeatedly in his mind and had convinced himself that other colleagues had shown boredom with him on other occasions.

Not only was Jason's recollection of other situations false, but his interpretation of immediate situation was inaccurate because the yawn was not a response to Jason's presentation. His automatic thought was essentially irrational, because he selectively attended to information shaped by his core beliefs related to inadequacy. Replaying the initial interaction in his mind made him perceive mistakes he never made, magnifying his emotional response. Providing psychoeducation about this ruminative secondary process and encouraging the use of mindfulness skills can be beneficial for perfectionist patients.

Pie Charts

Like cognitive conceptualization diagrams and thought logs, pie charts are helpful visual tactics that allow patients to visually evaluate perfectionistic beliefs. For example, Jason felt his girlfriend would leave him if he performed poorly sexually. He believed that if he failed, the relationship could crumble. I gave him an assignment to assess four components of his relationship with his girlfriend that he felt were important to her (Greenberger, 1995). He came up with humor, emotional understanding, honesty, and sex. I then asked him to assess how important he thought these components were to his girlfriend, dividing them up as percentages. Figure 7.1 illustrates what he came up with.

Visually having this guide to look at helped Jason soften his perfectionistic beliefs about sex and place less emphasis on being perfect in that realm.

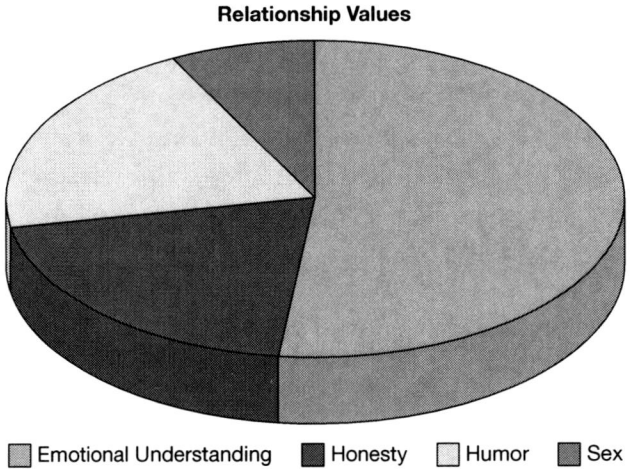

FIGURE 7.1 *Relationship Values. Jason's division of how important each of four relationship components was to his girlfriend.*

Behavioral Experiments

Another useful cognitive technique involves behavioral experiments. Behavioral experiments consist of having clients test theories about their beliefs by receiving responses from others in their daily environment (Beck, 1995). Jason, who was extremely preoccupied with his physical appearance and quite dissatisfied with how he looked, believed at times that he was overweight—despite being 6 feet 1 inch tall and weighing 175 pounds. When asked what actor he felt he looked like, Jason stated that he feared he resembled Paul Giamatti, a film actor who is overweight. Jason's homework was to ask peers what actor they felt he resembled to see whether they had the same impression. In the process of doing this survey, Jason learned that most people believed he looked like tall, usually slender actor Tom Hanks, which Jason was pleased with. No one felt he looked like Giamatti. Jason reported that doing the experiment was enjoyable and humorous, because he was able to see how distorted his beliefs have been.

I gave Jason additional experiments, including purposely making small mistakes on memos or asking for directions to places. These behavioral exposure experiments debunked ideas that he had to be perfect to keep others from noticing what he deemed to be imperfections. It also illustrated that he could survive mistakes and that making small mistakes did not have grave impacts or result in negative consequences.

EIGHT

Conclusion: Major Themes in Treating Perfectionist Clients

A great deal of research has illustrated that perfectionism is a trait that can make patients vulnerable to various psychiatric disorders, such a depression, anxiety suicide, and various personality disorders (Hewitt & Flett, 1993; Hewitt et al., 1992; Juster et al., 1996). Although, there is extensive research on how perfectionism can lead to psychopathology (Flett & Hewitt, 2002), there are few studies or books on how to treat perfectionists in a psychotherapeutic setting. This book is intended to help therapists address the clinical needs of perfectionist patients.

There are several components of how perfectionism is conceptualized. Hewitt and Flett's (1991) multidimensional perfectionism conceptualization has been one of the most widely popular and accepted constructs in and by the research community. As explained in Chapter 1, their conceptualizations consist of three subtypes of perfectionism: self-oriented perfectionism, socially oriented perfectionism, and other-oriented perfectionism.

Self-oriented perfectionism consists of an individual having excessively high goals or standards. This component of perfectionism may not be problematic and in some respects is adaptive. However, self-oriented perfectionists' relationship to their goals can lead to pathology. An intensely self-punitive attitude toward failure makes self-oriented perfectionists prone to experiencing extensive distress when their goals are unmet.

Socially oriented perfectionists are described as individuals who perceive that others have excessively high standards for them. This may lead them to squelch their needs while attempting to please others. In addition, anger and resentment may build toward others and be expressed passively or directly as they feel oppressed by the demands they feel they need to fulfill. Their tendency to please others often causes others to expect them to forgo their own needs, thus creating a self-fulfilling prophecy.

Other-oriented perfectionists have extremely high expectations of others. People may perceive them as difficult to please and feel as though they are "walking on eggshells" when interacting with people who display this subtype of perfectionism. When others fail to meet their expectations, other-oriented perfectionists can become punitive. This dynamic can greatly affect interpersonal relationships.

Therapists often find it extremely challenging to form a positive therapeutic alliance with patients who have perfectionist traits (Zuroff et al., 2000). This may be related to perfectionists' tendency to avoid expressing vulnerabilities or what they deem to be imperfections (Hewitt et al., 2003). This lack of disclosure can leave them relating in an emotionally disconnected fashion to therapists. Specifically, perfectionist patients may refrain from discussing the most important issues they need help with when in therapy. Some perfectionist patients (socially oriented) may also fear that not accommodating their expectations of the therapist's desires will threaten the relationship. Other perfectionists (other oriented) may be hypercritical and have unrealistic expectations about how their therapist should perform.

In addition to obstacles that perfectionist patients pose interpersonally, they may have an extremely punitive stance toward themselves (self-oriented). This rigid orientation makes responding to feedback extremely difficult. Feedback in the therapy relationship may be experienced as a slight, resulting in anger that may be expressed directly or indirectly (Besser, Flett, & Hewitt, 2004).

Chapter 2 discussed approaches for building the therapeutic alliance and working effectively with perfectionist patients. The following techniques were suggested:

1. *Providing psychoeducation.* For example, when working psychodynamically, discussing the concept of the observing ego can help perfectionist patients obtain the proper distance to possibly expose vulnerabilities in a less inhibited fashion. As the role of joining with the therapist collaboratively is described, the therapeutic process of analyzing self-behavior may become more normalized.
2. *Assessing costs and benefits of perfectionism.* Acknowledging the positive aspects of perfectionism validates the patient's current coping style. Simultaneously discussing how perfectionism may be negative and interfere with long-term goals lays the groundwork for considering and motivating change (motivational interviewing) due to the creation of cognitive dissonance.
3. *Decreasing self-estrangement.* Patients who are disconnected with how they feel about engaging in perfectionistic behaviors can become more conscious of how they suppress these feelings.
4. *Identifying ruptures.* Therapeutic ruptures that go unaddressed can erode the therapy relationship and lead to premature terminations. Withdrawal ruptures occur when patients indirectly express displeasure with the therapist and process (Safran & Muran, 2000). This may be prevalent with socially oriented perfectionists. Helping these patients directly communicate their needs rather than accommodating them can lead to psychological growth. In contrast, confrontational ruptures can be

transparent (Safran & Muran, 2000). Identifying hurt feelings behind the direct frustration can help perfectionists reveal vulnerabilities.

Subsequent chapters give examples of ruptures and ways to manage and understand perfectionist patients from diverse perspectives (interpersonal, self-psychological, and Kleinian). These perspectives focus on the relationship between the therapist and the patient. From these psychodynamic perspectives, change takes place by working through enactments that are replayed in the therapy relationship. Such enactments help patients develop new ways of interacting.

From an interpersonal perspective, keep in mind the following key elements, detailed in Chapter 3, when working with perfectionist patients:

1. *Validating the patient's perception of the therapist's countertransference.* If the patient feels the therapist is withholding and the therapist agrees, responding transparently can help the patient feel affirmed and more inclined to discuss the relationship. The therapist's acknowledgment of the patient's perspective, as well as acknowledgment of his or her own mistakes in the therapy relationship, can help model for the patient that imperfections can be tolerated.
2. *Jumping to conclusions.* Initially asking questions about how the patient is feeling is more helpful than providing feedback about the therapist's perception of the patient's emotional state.
3. *Allowing communication transparency.* Explaining the rationale for certain questions or interpretations can decrease a perfectionist patient's vulnerability as the therapist's way of communicating becomes more normalized.
4. *Joining.* Working with a perfectionist patient's defense, rather than challenging it, results in a stronger therapeutic relationship until safety in that relationship has been established.

5. *Showing nonverbal awareness and communication.* Paying attention to nonverbal behavior and bringing it to the patient's attention can expand awareness.
6. *Providing metaphors.* When interacting with perfectionist patients, metaphors can help the patients receive feedback receptively.

As with an interpersonal perspective, a self-psychological framework requires paying attention to what is enacted in the therapy relationship. The valuable self-psychology aspect of shifting listening perspectives can be beneficial when working with perfectionist patients. These perspectives are referred to as subject-centered listening and other-centered listening (Fosshage, 1997). Subject-centered listening focuses on the patient's perspective, during which the therapist strives to understand the patient's subjective experience and asks, "What does the patient need from me?" This perspective is employed when the patient is feeling less cohesive and sturdy.

When the patient's self-state is stable, other-centered listening may be appropriate and helpful. Other-centered listening focuses on how the therapist feels about an interaction. The key question is "How is the patient making me feel?" or "What is happening between us in this therapy relationship?" Other-centered listening is useful in ascertaining how a patient may contribute to interpersonal dynamics with other people. Paying attention to the patient's self-state and shifting listening to accommodate the self-state can foster the connection and help the patient overcome therapeutic ruptures.

Important points from Chapter 5 are using Klein's paranoid–schizoid and depressed positions (Segal, 1974). These fluctuating positions can be used to monitor patients' levels of functioning and listen to them with a valuable framework informing the therapist about how to intervene. In the depressed position, patients experience guilt feelings due to fear of their aggression toward others (mental representations) that they love. Helping patients understand and communicate this ambivalence can be beneficial. As feelings of guilt are discussed, the perfectionists' (particularly social oriented) anxiety about expressing their needs can be better tolerated.

Conversely, in the paranoid–schizoid position, patients may fear retaliation from aggressive or envious attacks (Segal, 1974). This aggression may protect perfectionist patients' sense of omnipotence and protect against threats to their sense of self. Understanding this dynamic can help patients survive the aggression and work through rigid mind sets. When patients are in the paranoid–schizoid position, subject-centered listening can often be useful, because these patients' self-state is fragmented.

In general, because perfectionism is a persistent trait rather than an isolated symptom, research suggests that long-term psychodynamic therapy (interpersonal, self-psychological, or Kleinian) that focuses on personality change and the therapy relationship is recommended (Blatt et al., 1996). However, this does not mean that mindfulness and cognitive therapy techniques cannot be used, as Chapters 6 and 7 explain.

Mindfulness is a technique that is similar to the observing ego described in Chapter 2. Through the practice of mindfulness, patients learn to apply this skill and build reflective functioning. This reflective functioning can be applied when examining reactions that emerge in the therapy relationship, as well as other interpersonal interactions. Consequently, mindfulness skills can be superimposed onto psychodynamic approaches. In addition, mindfulness exercises focusing on building compassion can mitigate the punitive stance perfectionists take toward themselves and others.

For patients initially threatened about focusing on the interpersonal dynamic of therapy, Mindfulness and cognitive therapy techniques, such as cognitive restructuring, can be implemented to build ego strength. Once skills are strengthened, perfectionist patients may have the capacity to delve into a deeper therapeutic endeavor.

Overall, working with perfectionist patients is extremely complicated, requiring skills and understanding of diverse psychotherapeutic frameworks. At times, I have feelings of incompetence, fear I am not living up the expectations of perfectionist patients, or feel hurt when attempting to manage aggressive outbursts. Understanding my personal reactions, as well as the dynamics of perfectionism, has helped me remain empathic and strive to be good enough. Being okay with "good enough" is, in a way, what I hope my perfectionist patients will learn to tolerate.

References

Aldea, M. A., Rice, K. G., Gormley, B., & Rojas, A. (2010). Telling perfectionists about their perfectionism: Effects of providing feedback on emotional reactivity and psychological symptoms. *Behaviour Research and Therapy, 48*, 1194–1203.

American Psychiatric Association. (1994). *Diagnostic and statistical manual of mental disorders* (4th ed.). Washington, DC: Author.

Bastiani, A. M., Rao, R., Weltzin, T., & Kaye, W. H. (1995). Perfectionism in anorexia nervosa. *International Journal of Eating Disorders, 17*, 147–152.

Besser, A., Flett, G. L., & Hewitt, P. L. (2004) Perfectionism, Cognition and Affect in response to performance failure vs sucesss. *Journal of Rational-Emotive & Cognitive Behavior Therapy, 22*, 301–328.

Beck, J. S. (1995). *Cognitive therapy: Basics and beyond*. New York, NY: Guilford Press.

Blatt, S. J., Zuroff, D. C., Quinlan, D. M., & Pilkonis, P. A. (1996). Interpersonal factors in brief treatment of depression: Further analyses of the National Institute of Mental Health Treatment of Depression Collaborative Research Program. *Journal of Consulting and Clinical Psychology, 64*, 162–171.

Bordin, E. (1979). The generalizability of the psychoanalytic concept of the working alliance. *Psychotherapy: Theory, Research, and Practice, 16*, 252–260.

Dunkley, D. M., Blankstein, K. R., Halsall, J., Williams, M., & Winkworth, G. (2000). The relation between perfectionism and distress: Hassles, coping, and perceived social support as mediators and moderators. *Journal of Counseling Psychology, 47*, 437–453.

Dweck, C. S. (2012). *Mindset: How you can fulfill your potential*. London, England: Constable & Robinson.

Enns, M. W., Cox, B. J., & Clara, I. P. (2005). Perfectionism and neuroticism: A longitudinal study of specific vulnerability and diathesis-stress models. *Cognitive Therapy and Research, 29*, 463.

Epstein, M. (1996). *Thoughts without a thinker: Psychotherapy from a Buddhist perspective*. New York, NY: Basic Books.

Flett, G. L., Besser, A., Davis, R., & Hewitt, P. L. (2003). Dimensions of perfectionism, unconditional self-acceptance, and depression. *Journal of Rational-Emotive and Cognitive-Behavior Therapy, 2*, 119–138.

Flett, G. L., & Hewitt, P. L. (2002). *Perfectionism: Theory, research and treatment*. Washington, DC: American Psychological Association.

Fosshage, J. (1997). Listening/experiencing perspectives and the quest for a facilitative responsiveness. In A. I. Goldberg (Ed.), *Progress in self psychology* (Vol. 13, pp. 33–55). Hillsdale, NJ: Analytic Press.

Frost, R. O., Heimberg, R. G., Holt, C. S., Mattia, J. I., & Neubauer, A. L. (1993). A comparison of two measures of perfectionism. *Personality and Individual Differences, 14*, 119–126.

Frost, R. O., Marten, P., Lahart, C., & Rosenblate, R. (1990). The dimensions of perfectionism. *Cognitive Therapy and Research, 21*, 209–232.

Greenberg, J. R., & Mitchell, S. A. (1983). *Object relations in psychoanalytic theory*. Cambridge, MA: Harvard University Press.

Greenberger, D., & Padesky, C. A. (1995). *Mind over mood: Change how you feel by changing the way you think*. New York, NY: Guilford Press.

Harding, M., Hewitt, P., & Flett, G. (2003). Perfectionism, coping, and quality of intimate relationships. *Journal of Marriage and Family, 65*, 143–158.

Hewitt, P. L., & Flett, G. L. (1991). Perfectionism in the self and social contexts: Conceptualization, assessment, and association with psychopathology. *Journal of Personality and Social Psychology, 60*(3), 456–470.

Hewitt, P. L., & Flett, G. L. (1993). Dimensions of perfectionism, daily stress, and depression: A test for the specific vulnerability hypothesis. *Journal of Abnormal Psychology, 102*, 58–65.

Hewitt, P. L., Flett, G. L., & Turnbull, W. (1992). Perfectionism and multiphasic personality inventory (MMPI) Indices of personality disorder. *Journal of Psychopathology and Behavioral Assessment, 14*(4), 323–335.

Hewitt, P. L., Flett, G.L., Turnbull-Donovan, W. (1992). Perfectionism and suicide potential. *British Journal of Clinical Psychology, 31*(2), 181–190.

Hewitt, P. L., Flett, G. L., Turnbull-Donovan, W., & Mikail, S. F. (1991). The multidimensional perfectionism scale: Reliability, validity and psychometric properties in psychiatric samples. *Psychological Assessment: A Journal of Consulting and Clinical Psychology, 3*, 464–468.

Hewitt, P. L., Habke, A. M., Lee-Baggley, D. L., Sherry, S. B., & Flett, G. L. (2008). The impact of perfectionistic self-presentation on the cognitive, affective, and physiological experience of a clinical interview. *Psychiatry, 71*(2), 93–122.

Hewitt, P. L., Sherry, S. B., Habke, M., Parkin, M., Lam, R., McMurty, B., & Stein, M. B. (2003). The interpersonal expression of perfection: Perfectionistic self-presentation and psychological distress. *Journal of Personality and Social Psychology, 8*, 1303–1325.

Isaacson, W. (2011). *Steve Jobs*. New York, NY: Simon and Schuster.

Juster, H., Heimberg, R. G., Frost, R. O., Holt, C. S., Mattia, J. I., & Faccenda, K. (1996). Social phobia and perfectionism. *Personality and Individual Differences, 21*, 403–410.

Kabat-Zinn, J. (1994). Wherever you go. There you are: Mindfulness Meditation for Everyday Life. Hyperion.

Kilbert, J. J., Langhinrichsen-Rohling, J., & Saito, M. (2005). Adaptive and maladaptive aspects of self-oriented versus socially prescribed perfectionism. *Journal of College Student Development, 46*, 141–156.

Kohut, H. (1971). *The analysis of the self: A systematic approach to the psychoanalytic treatment of narcissistic personality disorders*. Madison, CT: International Universities Press.

Kohut, H. (1984). *How does analysis cure?* Chicago, IL: University of Chicago Press.

Kornfield, J. (2008). *The wise heart: A guide to the universal teaching of Buddhist philosophy*. New York, NY: Bantam.

Lennon, J., & McCartney, P. (1969). *The End. On Abbey Road* [CD]. London, England: Apple.

Levenson, E. A. (1983). *The fallacy of understanding & the ambiguity of change*. New York, NY: Basic Books.

Linehan, M. M. (1993). *Skills training manual for treating borderline personality disorder*. New York, NY: Guilford Press.

Melrose, S. (2011). Perfectionism and depression: Vulnerabilities nurses need to understand. *Nursing Research and Practice*. Article ID 858497, doi:10.1155/2011/858497: 2.

Mitchell, S. (1988). *Relational concepts in psychoanalysis: An Integration*. Cambridge, MA: Harvard University Press.

Mitchell, S. A., & Black, M. J. (1996). *Freud and beyond: A history of modern psychoanalytic thought*. New York, NY: Basic Books.

Nakano, K. (2009). Perfectionism, self efficacy and depression: Preliminary analysis of the Japanese version of the almost perfect scale revised. *Psychological Reports, 104*(3), 896–908.

O'Connor, D. B., O'Connor, R. C., & Marshall, R. (2007). Perfectionism and psychological distress: Evidence of the mediating effects of rumination. *European Journal of Personality, 3*, 429–532.

Ogden, T. (1986). *Matrix of the mind.* Northdale, NJ: Jason Aronson, Inc.

Rhéaume, J., Freeston, M. H., Dugas, M. J., Letarte, H., & Ladouceur, R. (1995). Perfectionism, responsibility and obsessive–compulsive symptoms. *Behaviour Research and Therapy, 33*, 785–794.

Safran, J. D., & Muran, J. C. (2000). *Negotiating the therapeutic alliance: A relational treatment guide.* New York, NY: Guilford Press.

Segal, H. (1964). *Introduction to the work of Melanie Klein.* London, England: Hogarth.

Shahar, G., Blatt, S. J., Zuroff, D. C., Krupnick, J., & Sotsky, S. M. (2004). Perfectionism impedes social relations and response to brief treatment of depression. *Journal of Social and Clinical Psychology, 23*, 140–154.

Shapiro, D. (1999). *Psychotherapy of neurotic character.* New York, NY: Basic Books.

Sherry, S. B., Hewitt, P. L., Gordon, F. L., Lee-Baggley, D. L., & Hall, P. A. (2007). Trait perfectionism and perfectionistic self-presentation in personality pathology. *Personality and Individual Differences, 42*(3), 477–490.

Sherry, S. B., Law, A., Hewitt, P. L., Flett, G. L., & Besser, A. (2008). Social support as a mediator of the relationship between perfectionism and depression: A preliminary test of the social disconnection model. *Personality and Individual Differences, 45*(5), 339–344.

Sullivan, H. S. (Ed.). (1953). *The interpersonal theory of psychiatry.* New York, NY: W. Norton.

Ulu, I., & Tezer, E. (2010). Adaptive and maladaptive perfectionism, adult attachment, and big five personality traits. *Journal of Psychology, 144*(4), 327–340.

Wachtel, P. L. (2008). *Relational theory and the practice of psychotherapy.* New York, NY: Guilford Press.

Wang, K. T., Yuen, M., & Slaney, R. B. (2009). Perfectionism, depression, loneliness, and life satisfaction: A study of high school students in Hong Kong. *Counseling Psychologist, 37*(2), 249–274.

References

Williams, M., Teasdale, J., Segal, Z., & Kabat-Zinn, J. (2007). *The mindful way through depression: Freeing yourself from chronic unhappiness.* New York, NY: Guilford Press.

Zuroff, D. C., Blatt, S. J., Sotsky, S. M., Krupnick, J. L., Martin, D. J., Sanislow, C. A. 3rd., & Simmens, S. (2000). Relation of therapeutic alliance and perfectionism to outcome in brief outpatient treatment of depression. *Journal of Consulting and Clinical Psychology, 68*(1), 114–124.

Index

adaption, perfectionism and, 4–8
adequate self-mirroring
    responses, 58
affirmation/validation,
    needs for, 57
age-appropriate response, 58
aggression, 77
  anger and, 87
  level of, 31
  self-directed, 78
  and sense of badness, 77
annihilation
  sense of badness and, 77–78
  sense of destruction and, 78
anxiety
  depression and, 8, 10, 84
  interpersonal, 11–12
  level of, 36
  narrow style and defenses
    against, 38
attitude, change in, 69–71
attributional comments, 50–52
attributional interpretations, 50–51
automatic thoughts, 108, 109,
    112–114
awareness, lack of, 94

behavior
  hostile, 9
  and pathology, 35–37

behavioral change, treatment
    and, 37–39
behavioral experiments, 115–116
beliefs, 107–109, 112
breathing exercises, 97, 100
Buddhist-influenced techniques,
    mindfulness and, 93–106

children, phase-appropriate
    idealizing responses to, 58
cognitive-behavioral
    therapy, 15, 18
cognitive conceptualization,
    108–110
cognitive restructuring, 112–114
cognitive therapy
  pathology of, 107–110
  treatment of, 110–116
comments, attributional, 50–52
communication, 56
  nonverbal awareness and, 55
  strategies, 51
  therapeutic demeanor and
    stance, offering, 52–53
  therapist's countertransference,
    patient's perception of, 52
  transparency, 53–54, 120
compassion, mindfulness and,
    103–106

conceptualization, six-dimensional, 4
conflict, 25–26
confrontational styles, 30
confrontation markers, 31, 33
confrontation ruptures, 25, 30–32
cons of perfectionism, pros and, 22
contemporary interpersonal
    theorists, 37
core beliefs, 107–109, 112
costs and benefits,
    perfectionism, 119
countertransference
  mindfulness and, 102–106
  therapist's, 120
craving, 94, 98–100

depressed position
  Klein's, 80–81
  patient's apparent
    functioning in, 89
depression, 8, 10, 96, 121
  and anxiety, 8, 10, 84
dialectical thinking, 111–112
disclosure, lack of, 118
dukkha and causes, 94–95
dysfunctional attitude scale, 14

emotions
  deny, 96
  negative, 45
  and psychological processes, 39
  reactivity and distress, 20
enactments, 39, 48–49
envy, 79–80

feelings
  accepting and embracing, 96–97
  thinking categories, 95–96
Frost's dimensions of perfection, 4

hostile behavior, withdrawing/
    engaging in, 9

idealizing needs, 58–60
imperfections
  acknowledgement, 92
  motivation to avoid, 13
  nondisclosure of, 11
individuals with
    mirroring-deficient
    experience, 59
intermediate beliefs,
    107–109, 112
internalization of self-object
    relationship, 73
interpersonal approach, 75
interpersonal behavior
  engaging in, 36
  restricted, 37
interpersonal dynamics, 48
interpersonal exchanges, client and
    therapist engage in, 37
interpersonal psychotherapy,
    39, 81
interpersonal school, 91
interpersonal theory, 35, 36
interpretations, 50
intimate and therapy
    relationships, 12–15
irrational automatic thoughts,
    112–114

Kleinian school, 91
Kleinian theory, 77
  depressed position, 80–81
  paranoid–schizoid
    position, 78–80
  treatment and behavioral
    change, 81–90

layers, beliefs, 107–108
listening perspectives,
  66, 67, 76, 91
  shifting, 71
long-term intimacy, 72
long-term psychodynamic
  therapy, 122
long-term therapy, 14–15

maladaptation, perfectionism
  and, 8–10
meta-communication, 31
metaphors, 55, 121
mindful breathing, 97
mindfulness, 15, 122–123
  and compassion, 103–106
  and countertransference,
    102–106
  meditation, treatment and, 95–102
    accepting and embracing
      feelings, 96–97
    anger, embracing, 100–102
    craving, 98–100
    staying in moment, 97
    thinking categories, 95–96
mirroring-deficient experience,
  individuals with, 59
mirroring responses, 65
  types of, 58
multidimensional perfectionism
  conceptualization, 117

Narcissus, myth of, 95
negative emotions, 45
negative mood, 112
noble truths, 93–95
nonverbal awareness and
  communication, 55, 121
nonverbal behavior, 54

object constancy, 76
obligation/delay, 9
other-centered listening,
  66–67, 121
other-oriented perfectionists,
  3, 118
  associated with externalizing
    personality pathology, 11
  craving, 94

paranoid–schizoid position, 78–81,
  88, 122
  patient's apparent
    functioning in, 89
parental mirroring
  responses to child,
    appropriate, 58
pathology, 77
  behavior and, 35–37
  belief layers, 107–108
  cognitive conceptualization,
    108–110
  self-psychology and,
    59–60
patient's aggression, process of
  ameliorating, 31
patient's subjective experience, 32
perfectionistic self-presentation
  and personality disorders,
    11–12
phase-appropriate idealizing
  responses to children, 58
phase-appropriate mirroring
  response, 58
  lack of, 65
phobia, behavioral treatment
  for, 96–97
pie charts, treatments, 114–115
problem-solving approach, 68
pros and cons of perfectionism, 22

psychodynamic approaches, 76
    with perfectionists, integration of, 90–92
psychodynamic therapy, 18
    long-term, 122
psychoeducation, 18, 114, 119

qualified assertions, 27–28

reflective functioning, 122
relational therapist, 60, 75
repetitive dynamics, 39
resolution in relationships, lack of, 12
rumination, 10, 15
ruptures, 25
    confrontation, 25, 30–32
    disembedding process, 27
    identification, 26
    recognizing, 31
    resolving, 26
    stage model to manage, 26
    therapy. *See* therapy ruptures
    withdrawal, 25–28

secondary processing, 113–114
self-acceptance, lack of, 9
self-assertions, 28
self-directed aggression, 78
self-disclosure, 33
self-estrangement
    decreasing, 119
    therapy, 23–25, 29
self-fragmentation, 72
self-identity, 79
self-object relationship, internalization of, 73
self-oriented perfectionism, 3, 4, 45, 118
    associated with compulsivity, 11
    mixed traits of socially and, 43–49
    rumination, 10
self-oriented perfectionists, 24–25, 30, 80
    craving, 94
self-presentation, perfectionistic, 11–12
self-psychological framework, 121
self-psychological perspectives, 61, 74
self-psychological school, 91
self-psychological therapist, 60, 66
self-psychology, 81
    in comparison to other psychodynamic approaches, 75–76
    listening perspectives to foster change, 66–71
    and pathology, 59–60
    theory and development, 57–59, 66
    therapeutic interaction, 71–75
    treatment and behavioral change, 60–66
self-punishment, 22, 104
self-punitive, 22
self-verification theory, 20
sense of badness and annihilation, 77–78
six-dimensional conceptualization, 4
social dissatisfaction, 28–30
socially oriented perfectionists, 3, 24, 81, 118
    affecting marital relationships, 12–13
    associated with emotional dysregulation deficit, 11

craving, 94
maladaptation, 9
related to interpersonal anxiety and dependency, 12
rumination, 10
and self-oriented perfectionism, mixed traits of, 43–49
therapeutic action with, 39–42
social support, lack of, 9
subject-centered listening, 121, 122
perspectives, 66, 69

TDCRP. *See* Treatment of Depression Collaborative Research Program
therapeutic alliances, 2, 17, 20–23, 61
cognitive-behavioral therapy, 18
observing ego, 19–20
psychodynamic therapy, 18
rationale of therapeutic interventions, 19
self-presentation style and, 8
strengthening, 34
therapy relationship and, 13
therapeutic approach, 19
therapeutic demeanor and stance, 52–53
therapeutic interaction, internalizing, 71–75
therapeutic interventions, rationale of, 19
therapeutic process, 86
therapeutic ruptures, identification of, 119–120
therapeutic tests, 88–89
therapist, choosing, 67–69
therapist's countertransference, patient's perception of, 52, 120

therapist's subjective experience, 32
therapy relationships, 82
feedback in, 119
interventions and, 68–69
intimate and, 12–15
therapy ruptures, 25–26
confrontation ruptures, 30–32
discussing interaction, 32–34
social dissatisfaction, 28–30
therapeutic alliance, strengthening, 34
withdrawal ruptures, 26–28
thinking categories, 95–96
three-component conceptualization, 2–3
Treatment of Depression Collaborative Research Program (TDCRP), 14
treatments, 110
and behavioral change, 37–39
self-psychology, 60–66
behavioral experiments, 115–116
cognitive restructuring, 112–114
dialectical thinking, 111–112
and mindfulness meditation, 95–102
pie charts, 114–115

unconditional self-worth, 9–10
unmet idealizing needs, individuals with, 59

visualization and mindfulness, 96

withdrawal markers, 26
withdrawal ruptures, 25–28